Lamborghini Countach

Osprey AutoHistory

Lamborghini Countach

LP 500, LP 400, LP 400 S, LP 500 S, 5000
Quattrovalvole

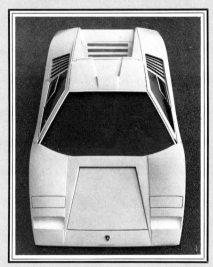

JEAN-FRANÇOIS MARCHET
& PETER COLTRIN

First published in 1981 by Osprey Publishing Limited
27A Floral Street, London WC2E 9DP
Member company of the George Philip Group
This revised edition published in spring 1986
First reprint early 1987
Second reprint early 1988

United States distribution by

Osceola, Wisconsin 54020, USA

British Library Cataloguing in Publication Data

Marchet, Jean-François
    Lamborghini Countach: LP 500, LP 400, LP 400 S,
    LP 500 S, 5000 Quattrovalvole——Rev. ed.——(Osprey
    AutoHistory)
    1. Countach automobile
    I. Title
    629.2′222   TL215.C6/

ISBN 0-85045-681-9

Associate Michael Sedgwick
Photography by the authors

Printed in England by
BAS Printers Limited, Over Wallop, Hampshire

Contents

Introduction:
The Supercar apart

The Lamborghini Countach can be considered as the Goddess of Supercars because of its styling, because of its technology, because of its strong character. Every enthusiast must agree that it is the most impressive car ever made. French motoring journalist Jose Rosinski once wrote in *Sport Auto:* 'Compared to the Countach, the fabulous Ferrari Boxer seems to have been manufactured for pot-bellied old men'. No comment.

It has to be admitted that the Countach is the only car you recognize immediately when you see it way back (for a few seconds...) in your rear-view mirror. It would be unfair to state that it is far better than the Ferrari Testarossa. These two Emilian *gran turismo* cars were designed with completely different states of mind. Less practical, less realistic, the Countach was inspired by aesthetics and performance only. Though it was born and developed during a long, troubled period which affected the factory, no concessions were made to these two intents.

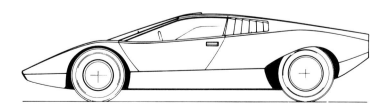

Ten years after its introduction the Countach seems to have found its balance. Yes, this car is more than ten years old; it was even designed 15 years ago. However, on the journey of passion, no other car can hold a candle to the Countach.

CHAPTER ONE

A man able to make his dreams come true

The Automobili Ferruccio Lamborghini S.p.A. was founded in 1963 near Bologna, at Sant'Agata Bolognese, not far from Modena in northern central Italy. After the success of the *Lamborghini Trattrice* (the farm tractor factory founded in 1949) and the *Lamborghini Bruciatori* (the ventilation equipment factory founded in 1960), *Cavaliere* Ferruccio Lamborghini had decided to come back to his first love—high-performance cars. In fact, the first Lamborghini car dated back some 15 years before, to 1948: it was simply a Fiat Topolino modified for racing! In 1963 Lamborghini wanted recognition, and no more so than for building the best GT car. It was not just because Ferruccio Lamborghini had been disappointed by the behaviour of his personal Ferraris, as has often been stated, it was because he was, first and foremost, a perfectionist.

One of the major problems was to have an all-Italian engine of top quality. Lamborghini, therefore, sought the help of Giotto Bizzarrini, who had been formerly employed by both Alfa Romeo and Ferrari, the latter for whom he had helped design the classic 250 GTO. Bizzarrini had left Maranello after the 'palace revolt' and was working at the time as a freelance. He had on his files a V12 cylinder engine, of four overhead camshafts, which was exactly what Lamborghini desired and

Kindred creative spirits looking young, eager and dapper, on the left Giampaolo Dallara. Ferruccio Lamborghini alongside does look young

needed, that is to say, a pure and more advanced design than the production Ferrari V12 with then only one camshaft per block. The only obstacle was that the engine had been conceived for Formula 1 racing and had therefore a capacity of only 1500 cc. Bizzarrini was put under contract and sent back to his drawing board, where he produced a 3.5 litre (77 × 62 mm, bore and stroke), of the same style suitable for series manufacture and street use.

The first engine components were cast with the assistance of the ATS smelting plant, and crankshafts were soon to be seen at the tractor factory at Cento. A tubular chassis was manufactured during the summer of 1963, while Franco Scaglione was charged with the body styling. The very

Architype Bolognese industrial site — the Lamborghini factory behind 'forever' railings and sliding gate. The first Wolf Countach ploughs, or should it read, dances in?

first Lamborghini would be ready in time for that November's Turin Show.

In June 1963, Ferruccio Lamborghini had engaged Giampaolo Dallara, a then 24-year-old engineer trained at Maserati and Ferrari. Dallara was instructed to develop the engine and the chassis of the first car, the 350 GTV. In that task, he was backed by 25-year-old Paolo Stanzani. The team was further reinforced by the arrival of New Zealander Robert Wallace (also a mere stripling of 25), who already had lots of experience as a racing mechanic. Bob was soon to be entrusted with road testing. No doubt these young gentlemen were hoping Lamborghini would go racing....

Ferruccio Lamborghini did not dislike motor racing, but he was wise enough not to tackle two jobs at once. Simply making the best GT car was already a big enough task. However, this did not prevent his young and enthusiastic team from burning the midnight oil on future plans. While the production 350 GT (and its immediate development, the 400 GT) was creating noticeable interest from customers, Dallara, Stanzani and Wallace were thinking of a 'super' *berlinetta* for racing.

Not only did Ferruccio Lamborghini receive their ideas without resentment, he showed himself delighted with their initiative. He gave them a frank 'go ahead', which lead to the TP 400 chassis, which was exhibited at the 1965 Turin Show. At that time, nobody would have guessed that this would mark the first step for what was to become one of the most famous cars in the world. Of course, this was to be the revolutionary Miura. By an incredible stroke of luck for Lamborghini, Carrozzeria Touring had suffered a financial upheaval which forced them to close their doors, thus driving the company into Bertone's arms. This association was going to produce some of the most beautiful cars ever made. It is fair to say that without Bertone the Miura would not have been as attractive and exciting as it is.

The Miura was more successful than Lamborghini dared expect. For the first time a 'dream' car had become a production model, with about 760 of these cars being made between 1966 and early 1973. However, in the materialistic and status-seeking world of the exotic car, people are always demanding more, and frequent updating of ideas is imperative if one wants to maintain one's position at the top.

In the early nineteen-seventies, Dallara left Lamborghini and went to DeTomaso to design a Formula 1 car. Stanzani was then asked to assume the dual role of chief engineer and plant manager at Sant'Agata. This dual role would not be an easy one, and Stanzani was going to face a tremendous number of problems he would not under normal circumstances encounter. Understandably, he too was going to throw in the sponge a few years later. Perhaps the worst of these troubles was the constant conflict between management, workers and government already afflicting the whole of Italy. Also there was the difficult birth of the Urraco, a smaller Lamborghini with a 2.5-litre V8 engine, which unfortunately was never to attain its objective as a serious competitor for Porsche's 911 and the Ferrari Dino.

However, Stanzani went on developing the Miura of which an ultimate version, the SV, was introduced at the 1971 Geneva Show. However, the star of the show was another Lamborghini: the Countach. Miura's daughter was taking her first steps.

CHAPTER TWO

Project 112

The Miura was still very much in demand and the latest SV received an ecstatic welcome. However, Stanzani and his design crew had come to the conclusion that by now the basic concept was getting a bit long in the tooth. They wanted to essay something new—and it was needed.

Initially given the code number 112, this project is now better known as 'Countach'. Like the Miura, the Countach was also far in advance of its time. Stanzani's objectives were better weight distribution and road holding. The Miura was criticized for being light at the front end at high speed. The Countach is not, but perhaps, reluctantly it has to be admitted, it is if anything a bit light at the rear, because of the demanding body shape. The new car would also have to be easier to drive. At the limit, the Miura was dangerous, a bit 'sharp' for an inexperienced driver arriving too quickly into a bend. Lifting off the throttle pedal under these conditions was very dangerous. Stanzani and his staff, which by then included the young and talented Massimo Parenti, opted, therefore, for a completely new and original chassis layout.

The successor to the Miura would obviously have to have an amidships engine. This is an ideal layout for an effective sports car in the futuristic idiom. Instead of a 'sidewinder' location, as the Miura, Stanzani's solution was to place the engine 'south to north', longitudinally with the

Out of fantasy came the fantastic—the Miura in the foreground lends a false perspective to the first LP 400 in the background. Picture too in your mind's eye the Ferrari 250GTO and Berlinetta Boxer alongside

gearbox but not the differential ahead of the engine. This would allow the five-speed gearbox to be right at the driver's elbow. Direct transmission shifting eliminates the need for control rods, which are not easy to design, build and adjust. But it did mean some very clever and complicated engineering.

The new layout called for a new sump, deeper and more heavily ribbed, as well as a new block casting. The gearbox position, ahead of the engine, entailed that there should be a drive-shaft driving back through a sealed lubrication chamber in the sump to the differential. According to test and other reports the expense was worth it. All the critics agree that shifting gears is a delight. The location of the engine also gave better directional stability and better accessibility to the ancillaries; distributors, alternator, water pumps and timing chains.

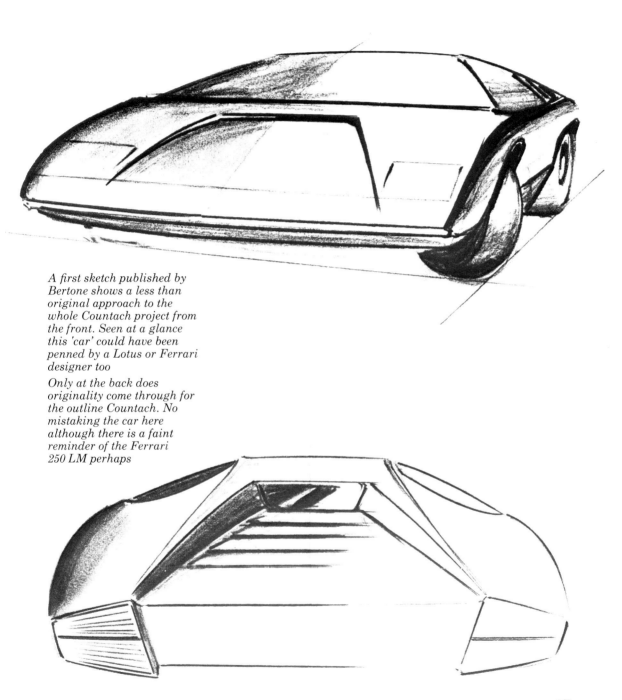

A first sketch published by Bertone shows a less than original approach to the whole Countach project from the front. Seen at a glance this 'car' could have been penned by a Lotus or Ferrari designer too

Only at the back does originality come through for the outline Countach. No mistaking the car here although there is a faint reminder of the Ferrari 250 LM perhaps

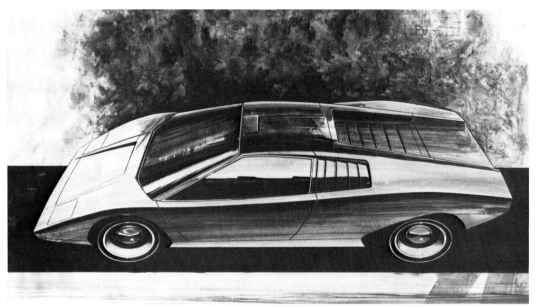

Above *When viewed from the
side for the first time, in full
'art drawing' style the overall
design impresses. Note the
intended periscope in the roof
and boring road wheels*

Stanzani, who was already working on bigger-displacement units for other Lamborghinis, intending to meet ever heightening emission regulations worldwide opted for a 5-litre engine. The engine had dimensions of 85 × 73 mm for a capacity of 4971 cc by contrast with the existing 3.9-litre type, with its bore of 82 mm and its 62 mm stroke. Plenty of power was recorded in the new dynomometer room (Schenck) built at around the same time. The factory released a figure of 440 bhp DIN at 7400 rpm and 366 ft lb at 5000 rpm with even higher outputs seen on test, but the engine structure posed a number of doubts as to long-term reliability. Thus, while the new block and sump were retained, these misgivings led to a reversion to the traditional dimension and 4-litre capacity on production cars.

Called the LP 500 (Longitudinal Posteriore 5

Below Once inside the magic really takes over. The early 'cutaway' immediately gives scale to the massiveness of the power train and its very close proximity to any fortunate driver. Rear body overhang becomes apparent too

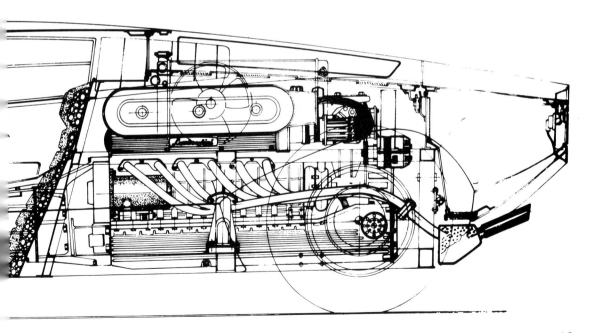

litri), the Countach was first intended merely as an experimental show car. Therefore, Stanzani developed a simple and straightforward chassis made of square tubes and welded-in panels. It was called a monocoque, but semi-monocoque is a closer description. Front and rear suspension were modified Lamborghini production units.

During this time, Marcello Gandini and his crew were creating one of the most impressive bodies ever to be made. We know that Bertone, like any other styling house, are reluctant to assign specific credit for authorship of their body designs, preferring to talk of team efforts. But in essence the Countach is one man's work: the creation of a master in his field. The name of Gandini has always received far less publicity than has Giorgetto Giugiaro, whom he replaced at Bertone, and is the well-known head of Ital Design, but nevertheless commands an equal degree of respect. Let us not forget that Gandini was responsible for all Lamborghini styling from 1966, including, of course, the Miura, which was the company's first masterpiece. He also designed the most impressive and striking show car of the nineteen-sixties, the Carabo, using Alfa Romeo mechanicals. This was the first car without a broken line from the bonnet to the end of the windscreen. Its doors, opening like beetle wings (*carabo*), were adopted on the Countach. Gandini was obviously given a *carte blanche* for the new Lamborghini coachwork.

As with so many styling exercises or show cars, the new Lamborghini LP 500 by Bertone was finished at the very last minute. When the car was ready, last thing at night, Bob Wallace took it over the mountain passes, snow and all, to Geneva in time for the eve of the Show. At that point the car had not yet been given a name. One of the Torinese workers engaged on the finishing

touches exclaimed '*Countach*' when he first saw it. This is a typical Piemontese slang expression, suggesting both astonishment and admiration. Anyway this is what legend would have us believe and the name somehow stuck.

This new Lamborghini was to have no link with fighting bulls. The only problem left was with its pronunciation, which is rarely made correctly. One should say 'Coontash', stressing the first syllable.

Still at Bertone, wind tunnel tests were initially carried out with a scale model of the LP 500 (to be) using the familiar 'string' tufts to record air flow

CHAPTER THREE

The first LP 500

Finished in a deep lemon yellow, the Lamborghini Countach began its eye-catching career at the 1971 Geneva Motor Show. The press coverage was tremendous, spreading far and wide within days, and in Japan the Countach soon became the favourite children's model car.

Of course, very few people were ready to believe that this incredible car would be put into production. 'Too futuristic, too way out', was overheard everywhere. However, all had forgotten that the same thing was said about the Miura in 1966.

Even on its stand at the Salon, the silhouette, only 1.03 m high, spelt high speed. Following a motor racing concept introduced on the Lotus 56 at Indianapolis, the Countach had a 'corner' profile, the front bonnet making a single line with the windscreen, notable for its extensive surface area. However, the smooth curves used on the body sides preserved some vestige of a traditional wing line. The Countach still looked like a car, contrary to what some traditionalists might think. The design of the rear wheel arches was considered outrageous, yet it is interesting to record that this motif is now mourned, since it was concealed on the later Countach S. Art, true art, is always in advance of its time. People quickly noticed that the LP 500 was not fitted with low-profile, wide racing tyres, which are very flattering. Instead, it had the 60 section tyre, developed

Above Back to pure fantasy for the first effort to style the dashboard. Unfortunately space age creative desire did not survive twentieth century practicalities of cost and manufacturing technique. This air brush art is worthy of note for its own sake

Below In reality the first Countach interior looked like this. The LP 500 somehow looked watered-down

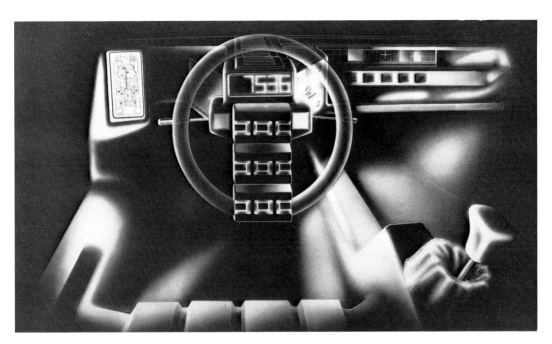

Above *What never fails to impress are the doors. The design and manufacturing cost of these alone, because of their obvious complexity, must frighten any insurance assessor. They are both practical and beautiful. This is the LP 500*

Right *Geometric precision. Note the slight 'radialling' of the intake slats either side of the engine, the neatness of the hinges for both doors and engine cover and the strong influence of the trapezium*

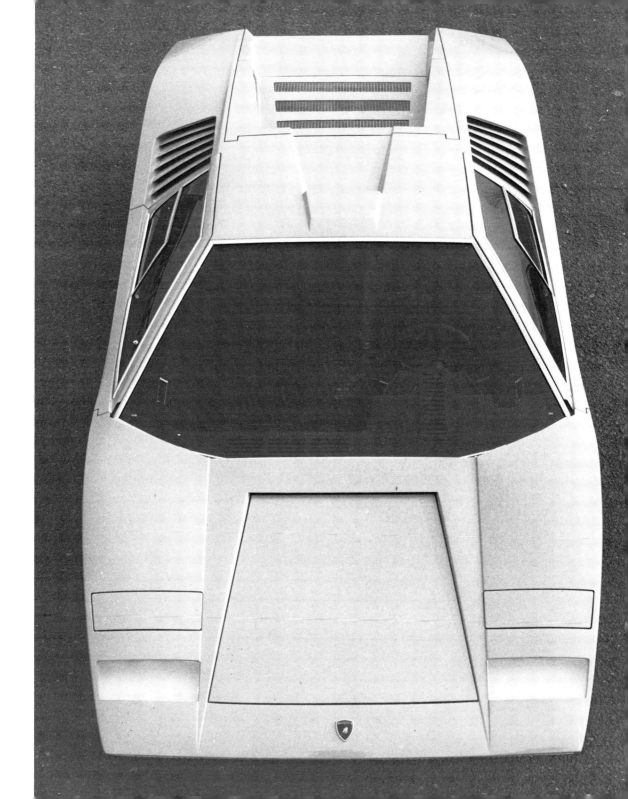

by Pirelli, and adopted on the Miura SV. The opening of the doors was very attractive.

Strictly speaking it is not a gull-wing system as the doors pivot in a direction parallel to the car, towards the nose, as on the Carabo. This was, however, the only similarity with the famous Bertone dream car. While the Carabo had a more complicated design with intensive use of louvres, the general shape of the Countach is very pure and clean. The headlamps are retractable and the direction indicators are hidden under Perspex covers as a reminder of traditional headlamps. The air intakes for cooling the engine replace side 'quarter-light' windows. The bonnet and nose

It's from the rear that the LP 500's form shows itself to be unbeatable. Trapeziodal influences ooze from every panel especially from the rear lamps and periscope. Even the lettering attempts to follow

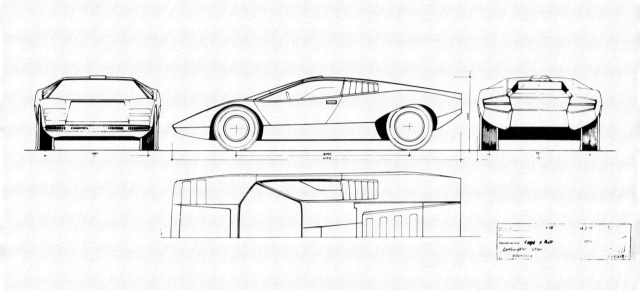

lines are unbroken by any inlet or outlet, while the rear-mounted radiators permit the use of a very thin nose-section. The ingenious use of trapeziodal forms is best appreciated from above. The body is basically a trapezium, divided into two other opposed trapezes which in their turn are also divided into trapezes. The first group comprises the bonnet and the windscreen; the second, the roof and engine compartment. Access to the engine is kept separated from the luggage boot. The bulge in the roofline is a fairing for the periscope device, which serves as the interior rear-view mirror.

Once one has opened the doors with the assistance of a servo hydropneumatic mechanism, it is possible to explore a futuristic interior treatment conceived with the aid of ideas from well-known Italian motoring journalist Gianni

A simplified press release scale drawing from Bertone. Their Coupe 2 posti *somehow loses its form when portrayed thus*

Rogliatti. A space-age readout instrument panel had been planned, but on this first car, things were a good deal simpler than might have been expected from the initial drawings. Already the digital speedometer and rev counter had been discarded, though they would later be adopted on Maserati's Quattroporte II—and run into considerable trouble, incidentally. The readout arrangement was meant to tell the driver how all the car's systems were working . . . or not working. However, apart from the traditional analogic rev counter and speedometer, only two big square warning lights were actually located on the steering column. The yellow one indicated minor problems, the red one . . . big problems! In both cases it was possible to evaluate the importance of the trouble thanks to a monitoring panel situated on the driver's left. This panel reproduced schematically all the functions of the car's various ancillaries. When in trouble, all the lights glowed permanently, with the exception of any one corresponding to a faulty part of the car. In fact, the lights glowing on the panel were no more than the warning lights shown on more normal production cars for oil pressure, headlamps, main beam. . . . Near the rev counter/speedometer were two other orange warning lights which glowed when exceeding a certain preset value on the instrument dials. In fact, these were the beginnings of cruise control! Bertone subsequently developed the use of electronic instrumentation on their dream cars. One of the most advanced was the Navajo, which had its rpm curve electronically metered on a linear scale, replacing the revolution counter. The instruments of the LP 500 were not very practical, but they marked an intriguing first step towards the true electronic dashboard. The warning light panel was a most attractive detail.

The overall interior design was clean and restrained. The one-spoke padded steering wheel complemented seats built up from two rows of rectangular pads. This layout recalled sports racers of the 1960s like Ferrari's P4 or the Ford GT40; the seats were rather narrow, of similar

LP 500 at the factory very close after it was finished, for all to admire. A typical Peter Coltrin shot for which he is so rightly famous

29

Finished. Uncluttered and pure without chin, arches or spoiler the LP 500 would be the only example thus totally unencumbered. Note the twin wiper arrangement and the tyre mixture; Michelin front, Pirelli rear

size, separated by a big transmission tunnel, flanked by two trimmed side pieces, a reminder of the fuel cells on racing models. The electric switches were located on the central console and to the right of the driver. In spite of the shorter wheelbase, the Countach had a roomier cockpit than the old Miura, as these dimensions show.

	LP 500	Miura
Interior width to elbow	1510 mm	1410 mm
Pedal to seat distance	1200 mm	1020 mm
Roof to seat distance	920 mm	880 mm
Dashboard to seat distance	1180 mm	980 mm
Trunk capacity	175 dm³	140 dm³

Single struts support the doors, engine cover and 'boot lid' in turn. Note that 'Countach' has been replaced by 'Lamborghini' on the tail

The very mass of the 5 litre engine and all its ancillaries is overwhelming but there is nothing unusual about the side radiators, throttle linkage, air cleaners and distributor. Even the dip stick is ready to hand

No dreaming collector can ever own the LP 500. Only this one was built, and after an intensive testing programme it was crashed into the wall for the sake of homologation and for the E-mark; sacrificed for the LP 400s that enthusiasts could then buy.

CHAPTER FOUR

Making a show car a production, dream car

Like many idea cars, the LP 500 had been built in a great hurry. It had not been seriously tested and many important details had not been taken into account. You can, of course, neglect many of the practical details on a show car, but you cannot on a production car, even on a very special one like the Countach.

It took a rather long time, close on three years, between the first display of the one LP 500 and delivery of the first LP 400 (a white car that went to Walter Wolf in 1974). Many changes had to be made in the show car to enable it to become a sound production car, and these took time, but also some other events at the factory conspired to delay the introduction of the LP 400 into the market.

For some reason that was never clearly explained, Ferruccio Lamborghini sold 51 per cent of his company shares to the Swiss Georges Rossetti. Maybe the founder was a little fed-up with his difficult-to-handle factory and its labour relations. However, he had already met his challenge and had produced some of the world's best GT cars. Did he need to do more? Perhaps he foresaw what would happen to the firm, a series of ups and downs in which the downs would far outnumber the ups. Maybe this same feeling led Bob Wallace to resign from the firm to which he

contributed so much just at the moment when the Countach was due to go into production. The birth of the LP 400 was going to be his last work as a loving midwife.

Subjecting the LP 500 prototype to an immediate and comprehensive test programme would have damaged it very quickly and thereby wrecked the factory's chances of decent promotion. Thus Bob Wallace had to wait for some time before being able to use the car quite freely.

Above *Engine cooling tests took some time. Here the radiators are being checked at Modena. The ugly air scoop just above the new NACA duct indicates the extent of the problem*

Left *New Zealander Bob Wallace sits pensively during a break. Already the car has been modified with NACA style duct and pop-rivet panel*

35

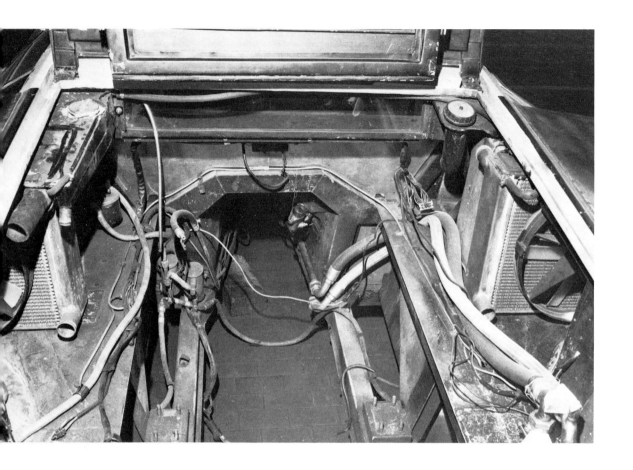

Inside the LP 500 showing considerable modification over the engine-installed shot earlier. The prototype has become dirty and obviously abused

Bertone also wanted it for their own promotional purposes. However, the first fast runs rapidly revealed that the improvised chassis was not so bad and that the road holding was quite promising. As soon as was possible, Bob arranged with Ing. Stanzani and Parenti for a detailed testing programme to start. This was to be carried out at the Modena Autodromo, the Varano di Melegari track and on the open road. The road course took in hilly stretches of the old Mille Miglia route between Bologna and Florence, which included

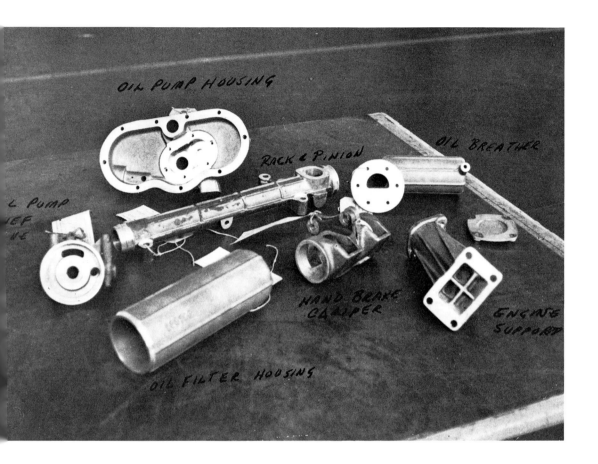

the Futa and Raticosa Passes, up in the hills. In May 1972, Wallace and Stanzani took the car to Sicily at Targa Florio time, not, of course, as competitors but simply to spectate. This 'spring holiday' combined business with pleasure, by subjecting the prototype to a shakedown cruise over everything from *autostrada* to the pot-holed tracks best suited to donkey-carts. Understandably, everything was done in the minimum possible time, yet the car did not miss a beat. Back at Sant'Agata, the car was fitted with a Telemax

Solid gold? Not quite, but close, because these Elektron castings are enormously expensive. Light and strong they, at least, symbolize an attempt to make the car both lighter in weight, and more exotic

37

The first LP 400 under construction. The chassis is massive and extremely strong, as come to that, is the engine. In fact the engine, showing off its four camshafts and vast 'sump' almost dwarfs the proceedings. It's July 1972

recording unit in the right footwell, and the development team, Ing, Parenti, Bob Wallace and Paolo Stanzani, continued their test on the Modena Autodromo. Wallace did most of the driving and one of his colleagues acted as observer-cum-calculator. For want of a proper wind tunnel at the works, recourse was made to wool tufts stuck along the body sides to study and

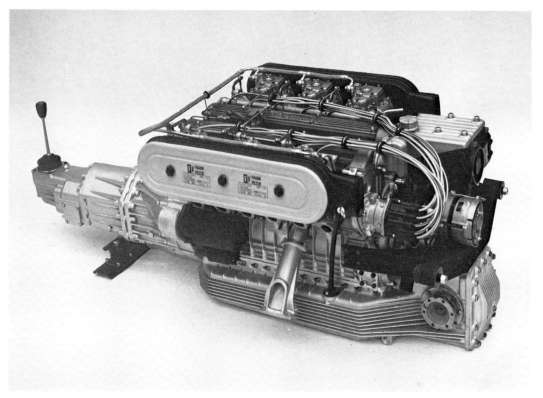

Above 'Back to front'. At one glance a beautifully compact, if massive, power train with unique crankshaft over 'driveshaft' arrangement. Each individual casting shows painstaking Italian craftsmanship

Left Transmission assembly is done slowly and carefully by hand. The crownwheel, displaying precision machining of finest quality, is driven by a hidden pinion and driveshaft which extends down the casing, sealed from the sump

LP 500 is destroyed to save the LP 400 series. The paintwork has been flattened off to enable satisfactory photography during the crash procedure. Look how strong the front end is. The driver's door has moved but has neither burst nor buckled

correct the aerodynamics. On the open road, the behaviour of these tufts was photographed from a second vehicle driving alongside.

Very early on, the main problem which manifested itself was the location of the radiators. Originally they were positioned one on each side of the engine bay, in a longitudinal layout. This caused severe overheating. A much more efficient arrangement was a transverse one, but this called

for larger air intakes over the rear wings. Various cooling airboxes were tested. The resultant design was not good for the pureness of Gandini's body shape, but the cooling of the engine demanded it, especially that of the 5-litre engine, which was much more prone to overheating. The resultant shape and effect were very satisfying and it would be even more so for the 4-litre version. Unlike the Miura, there were to be no

Because of the expense of the project extensive testing was done by the one prototype, LP 500. Other manufacturers would have built more cars. Here are more tufts to satisfy the company's aerodynamisists. There's nothing like testing in the flesh

problems of overheating with the production Countach.

The first results were excellent and Stanzani was soon to feel he had a winner with the Countach. The car's aerodynamic shape was every bit as good as it looked, showing less tendency to lift than the Miura and less sensitivity to side winds.

In accord with the wishes of the firm's then co-owners, Ferruccio Lamborghini and Georges Rossetti, Stanzani set down some guidelines for the production car. Firstly it had to be a true *macchina sportiva stradale*, a compromise between a smooth GT car and an aggressive sports car, capable of the standing-start kilometre in 23 seconds or less. It would be a cocktail of comfort, performance, stability and manoeuvrability. It would be a car for the true (driver) enthusiast, not just for mere seekers of the ultimate status symbol. Provision was to be made for air conditioning, but Ferruccio Lamborghini was unhappy about its actual installation, since it led not only to loss of power but also to a weight penalty. The car's weight needed to be reduced, and fighting the excess led to the use of many expensive materials and construction methods. Build cost was to be no object.

Sticking to the idea that 'weight is the enemy', but keeping strength in mind, Stanzani came up with a complicated-looking tubular space frame for the series production car. This was manufactured of Aq 40 extruded, normalized steel tube by Marchesi, a specialist frame-builder in Modena. The chassis, a true work of art in itself, accounts for a major part of the price tag. Unstressed aluminium panels were finally chosen for the body after Stanzani had investigated Avional, which, however, proved difficult to obtain and impossibly expensive. Another weight-saver was the use of thin but tough Gleverbel Belgian glass for the windscreen and windows. In its definitive form the car would come reassuringly close to the prescribed top limit of 1000 kilograms.

As part of the later development programme, the LP 500 was sent to England for homologation purposes, with tests at MIRA, the Motor Industry Research Association's testing laboratory. The final test required the car to be catapulted against a concrete wall. It was simply thought that if the one-off LP 500 passed, the even better built LP 400 would also fit the regulations. The choice of car may seem inept, but understandably Lamborghini was reluctant to destroy a brand new LP 400 as opposed to a well-used LP 500. Even Ferrari, with healthy Fiat backing behind them, have not been willing to stage crashes in order to comply with all the different regulations to be passed in

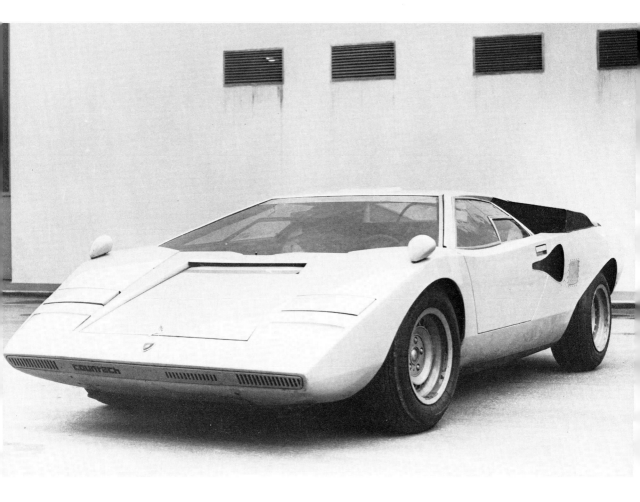

*Much testing now already
taken place but there's more
to go. LP 500 with exterior
changes. Note the nose, the
wing mirrors, scoops and
riveted panel. Already LP 500
looks tired*

obtaining homologation in different countries. As
much as they would like to sell all their cars in the
USA, only the Ferrari 308 type is approved there;
the Boxer and the 400 are not.

The big problem to solve in obtaining type
approval was the question of how to open the
doors if the car had overturned in an accident.
What could be done? One idea was to use aircraft-
type explosive door hinge bolts. This was deemed
a bit too drastic. Another idea was to have an

easily removable windscreen. However, it was decided to use ring-shaped linchpins to unhinge the doors if the car was in such an event. This way there could be no ham-handed mistakes caused by doors detaching themselves on the move. The linchpins cannot be accidentally pulled out. Nevertheless crashing a Countach is not a very nice experience at the best of times, especially when it catches fire. A rescued driver had told his story to one of the authors.

Rear view—dirty, tired and battered. Is that a Lucas number plate lamp above where a registration plate should be? Obviously that was forgotten previously. Note also the rivet line over the rear wing

45

CHAPTER FIVE

LP 400

The LP 400 took its bow at the Geneva Show in March 1973, with over two years having elapsed since the debut of the LP 500 prototype. Though very similar in shape, the Geneva LP 400, the first pre-production car, was, in fact, completely new.

From the outside, an experienced eye could notice a large number of differences between the 1971 (LP 500) and 1973 (LP 400) cars. First of all, after the relocation of the water radiators, some airboxes had been added on the rear wings, together with NACA air inlets in the doors. There were extra side windows near the airboxes; as yet they did not open, but for both technical and aerodynamic reasons the periscopic rear-view mirror had been forgotten. A new design of road wheel was fitted, closely approximating to the definitive version, now shod with Michelin XWX tyres. The nose was a little less sharp, including in it new air inlets for the front brakes. The tail lights had been replaced by more 'orthodox' ones fully framed in reflecting red plastic, and two windscreen wipers had been fitted. Inside, the dashboard was less exciting and yet more practical. The UFO instruments gave way to tiny American Stewart Warner gauges facing the driver and built into a kind of box. Six rectangular warning lights were fitted on the right. The design of the seats was much the same, but the centre channel went right up to the dashboard. Suede was extensively used for the interior trim.

One more detail: this first LP 400 was painted in Italian red and it looked magnificent. But let's go back to the technical details of the car.

The original mechanical layout remained un-changed, of course. As has been related the 5-litre engine lacked reliability, with an effective life of a mere 20,000 kilometres spoken of. For that reason, and maybe with a view to the use of parts common to the other V12 models in the then current

The wooden former from which the LP 400's panels were profiled. Obviously from the factory's experience with the LP 500 it was deemed essential to incorporate the NACA duct and large scoop for the side radiators. This time there has been a further change of nose detail

The first LP 400's interior forgot about the space age and went back twenty years. This time it was long on practicality (perhaps) and short on style. In this aspect alone this super supercar becomes something less

Lamborghini range, Stanzani reverted to the famous 4-litre unit. Power was transmitted from the end of the crankshaft via an aluminium Fichtel and Sachs clutch (similar to the Porsche 917 unit) to the five-speed, indirect-drive gearbox. From the gearbox's secondary shaft, power was transmitted to the drive shaft via a transfer gear. The drive shaft ran back through the engine sump to the ZF limited-slip differential at the engine's

The first LP 400's engine compartment has learned many things from the modified LP 500's. Those long side radiators have been replaced by the boxed ones featuring electric fans. The cam covers have also taken on that black wrinkled effect and the oil filler has changed

'rear end'. The shaft runs in two roller bearings and is sealed off from the sump, through which it passes, so that engine and gearbox are separately lubricated. The final drive ratio can be varied by changing the transfer gear rather than by varying crownwheel and pinion ratios. The sump and

Far left Hand assembly means lying on one's back. Here the rear suspension is built up into the chassis of an LP 400. Masking taped sheets of paper protect the alloy bodywork. Attractive Italian ceramic tiles provide a cold but suitable floor even in the most bland factories, making components and tools easy to find

Below left This factory cross-section drawing shows the simplicity of the LP 400's rear suspension. The hub carrier once more confirms the massiveness of the construction when viewed in profile with the coil spring over shock absorber. The anti-roll bar runs off to the right over the transmission

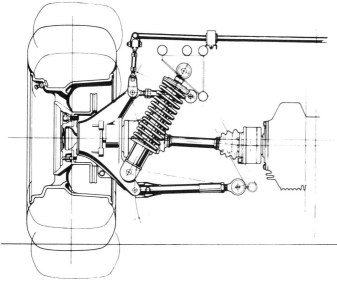

Left The front suspension cross-section is less explicit in this drawing. Note also the differences in A-arm angles, front to rear

A rare right hand drive production LP 400 sits at the factory awaiting delivery. More things have changed now—the wiper mechanism, the driving lamps by Carello, the side and flasher lights, side markers in the front wings and wing mirrors. Is that a 350 GT tucked behind the closed doors?

differential housing form a single, finned magnesium casting with separate compartments.

The Countach engine block was easily recognized by the waffle-like strengthening ribs on the lower block surroundings. Two six-plug Marelli distributors were adopted to replace the single 12-plug distributor used on the LP 500, although a single 70 amp alternator was adopted. Carburation remained basically unchanged, with six impressive horizontal Weber twin choke 45DCOE 23s.

The pressurized cooling system utilized two copper radiators, mounted vertically, one on each side of the engine, with a crossover connecting system. Air was drawn in at the sides through the waist-high intakes and NACA ducts, and exited aft through slotted grilles. Behind each radiator was an electrically driven fan; one automatically controlled by a thermostat and the other manually operated from the cockpit. By virtue of their location alongside the laterally mounted alloy fuel tanks, the radiators were close to the car's centre of gravity and so helped weight distribution. An oil radiator was located in the leading edge of the right front wing.

The front suspension was by unequal-length A-arms, or wishbones, with coil spring-over-shock absorber units and anti-roll bars located behind the axle line. Rear suspension was by single transverse upper links and lower A-arms, with each one's apex attached to the frame, plus two coil spring-over-shock absorber units per wheel. The shock absorbers were lightweight Koni units with aluminium cylindrical bodies, fully adjustable for bump and rebound and . . . very expensive. Front and rear hub carriers were magnesium castings; this arrangement proved unreliable since magnesium is prone to steady and gradual disintegration, and was dropped quite early in the production run. Lamborghini issued a memorandum advising owners to replace these hub carriers with new ones of light alloy. The brake components were derived from past racing experience—of others! They were Girling 18/4 discs with four pistons per caliper. The factory made their own rack-and-pinion steering gear with a magnesium housing. Stanzani had gone as far as was viable on the road car in his utilization of magnesium castings; for instance, on the sump, wheel uprights, engine mountings, camshaft covers, oil pump housing, handbrake caliper, gearbox casing, clutch housing and road wheels. Numerous other components were specially tailored for the Countach, not just adapted from mass-production units. Among these were the shock absorbers and the brakes, already mentioned, the ZF limited-slip differential and the clutch mechanism itself.

The red Geneva Show car, like the LP 500 before it, was later used for the road-test programme in Bob Wallace's hands, and another car, close to the definitive specification, was soon built. This second LP 400, still a pre-production car, was painted green (*Verde Countach*), but as yet lacked the dashboard in its final form, with control lights in the 'production' location. New air inlets under the chin of the car called for a slightly bigger nose, incorporating long-range driving lamps. The single windscreen wiper was of a more complicated parallelogram design than the prototype's twin blades. The front 'bumper' and window frames were still finished in aluminium and the side window openings were still as narrow as on the LP 500. This second car was displayed at the Paris Show later in 1973. The first true production car would not be ready before the 1974 Geneva Show.

The factory's press office published a detailed specification brochure for the LP 400 which we give in full on this spread and then overleaf. Compared with the information normally produced for such a car its content is nothing short of phenomenal. The stated top speed is 195 mph!

LAMBORGHINI COUNTACH LP 400

Marzo 1974

MOTORE

Sigla di fabbrica	L 406
Dimensioni, prestazioni:	
N. cilindri - disposizione	12 V (60°)
Diametro - corsa	82 x 62 mm (3.22 x 2.44 in.)
Rapporto corsa/diametro	0.75
Cilindrata unitaria	327.42 cm³ (19.97 cu. in.)
Cilindrata totale	3929 cm³ (239.7 cu. in.)
Area degli stantuffi	52.81 x 12 = 633.72 cm² (98.22 sq. in.)
Rapporto di compressione	10.5 : 1
Potenza massima	375 Cv. (DIN)
Regime di potenza massima	8000 giri/min
Potenza volumetrica	95 Cv/L (DIN)
Coppia massima	36.8 mkg (DIN 266 ft. lbs)
Regime di coppia massima	5500 giri/min
Regime massimo autorizzato	8000 giri/min
Senso di rotazione visto dal volano)	sinistrorso
p.m.e. max ($= \dfrac{Mt}{716.2} \cdot \dfrac{900}{V}$)	11 kg/cm² (156.2 lbs./sq in)
p.m.e. a regime potenza massima ($= \dfrac{Ne}{V} \cdot \dfrac{900}{n}$)	10.7 kg/cm² (151.9 lbs/sq. in)
Velocità media stantuffi a regime potenza massima	16.5 m/sec (54 ft/sec)
Peso a secco: motore solo	254 kg (559 lbs)
+ frizione (9 kg)	263 kg (578 lbs)
+ cambio (56 kg)	319 kg (702 lbs)
Rapporto peso/potenza:	
motore solo	0.65 kg/Cv (DIN)
propulsore completo	0.85 kg/Cv (DIN)
Potenza per unità di superficie dell'area stantuffi	0.59 Cv/cm² (DIN)
N. di ottano consigliato (NOR)	98-100

Costruzione

Posizione	centrale long
Materiale: monoblocco	lega leggera
teste	lega leggera
Canne cilindri: tipo	riportate umide
materiale	ghisa
Interasse cilindri	95 mm (3.74 in.)
Albero motore: materiale	acciaio al Ni-Cr-Mo temperato ad alta frequenza
Ø perni di manovella	43.604 mm (1.71 in.)
Ø perni di banco	62.979 mm (2.47 in.)
n. supporti di banco	7
Cuscinetti: di banco	bimetallici
di manovella	bimetallici
Bielle: materiale	acciaio
rapporto λ ($\dfrac{r}{L} = \dfrac{C}{2L}$)	0.387
Stantuffi: materiale	lega leggera
Fasce elastiche: materiale	ghisa
N.	3
segmenti compressione: tipo	cromato
segmenti raschia-olio: tipo	con molla ad elica
Coppie di serraggio dei bulloni principali (mkg/ft.lbs):	
Testa	8.6 kgm/72 ft.lbs
Testa bielle	6 kgm/43 ft.lbs

Cappelli banco ... 8 ... 12	2.8-9	kgm/20-65 ft.lbs
Cappelli assi a camme	2.8	kgm/20 ft.lbs
Collettore aspirazione/scarico	3	kgm/22 ft.lbs
Candele accensione	2.5-2.7	kgm/18-20 ft.lbs
Puleggia albero motore	2.8	kgm/20.8 ft.lbs
Bulloni volano motore	2.8	kgm/20 ft.lbs
Bulloni frizione	2.8	kgm/20 ft.lbs
Bulloni corona differenziale	7	kgm/51 ft.lbs

Distribuzione

N. valvole per cilindro		2
Posizione valvole		inclinate a V (70°)
Materiale valvole	aspirazione	acciaio
	scarico	acciaio
Materiale sedi valvole:	aspirazione	bronzo
	scarico	bronzo
Conicità sedi valvole:	aspirazione	45°
	scarico	45°
Diametro stelo valvole:	aspirazione	8 mm (0.31 in)
	scarico	8 mm (0.31 in)
Diametro testa valvole:	aspirazione	42 mm (1.65 in)
	scarico	38.2 mm (1.57 in)
Alzata valvole:	aspirazione	9.5 mm (0.39 in)
	scarico	8.4 mm (0.33 in)
N. e posizione alberi distribuzione		2 x 2 in testa
N. supporti assi a camme		4
Comando distribuzione		2 x 1 catena duplex
Fasatura:		
Aspirazione	inizio apertura	42° prima PMS
	fine chiusura	70° dopo PMI
	Durata apert.	292°
Scarico	Inizio apertura	40° dopo PMS
	fine chiusura	64° prima PMI
	Durata apert.	284°
Incrocio apertura valvole		82°
Giuoco valvole (a freddo):		
	aspirazione	0.25 mm (0.01 in)
	scarico	0.25 mm (0.01 in)

Accensione

Tipo		singola a batteria con 2 distributori e 2 x 1 bobine
Ordine di accensione		1-7-5-11-3-9-6-12-2-8-4-10
Numerazione cilindri		12 | 1
		11 | 2
		10 | 3
		9 | 4
		8 | 5
		7 | 6
		A ▼ V
Distributore		Marelli S 85 c.a.
Anticipo di calettamento		18°
Anticipo automatico		20°
	inizio	2200 giri/min
	fine	4500 giri/min
Giuoco tra i contatti ruttore		0.35 mm ± 0.05 (0.013'' ± 0.002'')
Candele		Bosch 235 P 21
Diametro e passo		14 x 1.25 mm
Distanza tra gli elettrolidi		0.35 mm (0.013'')

Alimentazione

Pompa alimentazione	2 Bendix elettr. 12 V
Portata pompa alimentazione	3.3 lt/min (0.72 imp. gals/min)
Carburatori: N. e sistema	6 doppio corpo orizzontali
marca e tipo	Weber 45 DCOE 96-97

Dispositivo partenza a freddo . .	
Regolazione carburatori:	
Diffusore	38 mm
Centratore	4.5 mm
Getto principale	1.50 mm
Getto minimo	45/F8
Getto pompa	0.35 mm
Corsa pompa	16 mm
Getto d'avviamento . . .	F 5/0.60 mm
Tubetto emulsionatore . .	F3
Getto aria di freno . . .	2.10 mm
Valvola a spillo	1.75 mm
Valvola aspirazione con foro di	
scarico	0.70 mm
Galleggiante	26 gr
Livellatura galleggiante . .	8.5 mm
Filtro aria N.	2 a secco
marca e tipo cartuccia	
filtrante	FIAAM FL-6248
Lubrificazione	
Tipo	forzata a carter umido
Pompa olio: N.	1
tipo	ad ingranaggi
* portata a 1000 giri/min	11 lt/min (2,4 imp. gals/min)
* press. a 1000 giri/min	2 kg/cm² (28.4 lbs/sq in)
a 6500 giri/min	7-8 kg/cm² (100-115 lbs/sq
a 90°C (105°F)	in)
Filtro olio: N.	1
marca e tipo cartuccia	
filtrante	FIAAM FA-0181
Radiatore olio	Flusso orizzontale
Raffreddamento	
Sistema	ad acqua
Pompa: tipo	centrifuga
portata a 1000 giri/min	12,6 litri/min
	(2,7 imp. gals/min)
a 6500 giri/min	94.2 litri/min
	(20.7 imp. gals/min)
Radiatori: flusso	orizzontale
taratura valvola tappo a	
pressione	0.9 kg/cm² (13 lbs/sq in)
pressione effettiva del	
circuito	1.09 kg/cm² (15.5 lbs/sq in)
Termostato: marca e tipo .	SAVARA - 0-10-034-00
localizzazione . .	su manicotto uscita teste
inizio apertura . .	70°C/172,4°F
Corsa	7.5 mm
Ventola: numero	2 assiali a 5 pale
funzionamento . .	1 elettrico
	1 elettrico a termocontatto
	tarato a 75° C (167° F)
Impianto elettrico	
tensione	12 V
batteria	66 Ah
alternatore	Bosch 70 A
distributore	S 85 c.a.
motorino avviamento . .	Bosch 12 V / 1.8 Cv

TRASMISSIONE

Frizione: tipo	monodisco a secco
Ø del disco	241,30 mm (9.5 in.)
tipo molla	diaframma
comando	idraulico
Cambio: posizione . . .	ant.
N. rapporti . . .	5 + RM
tipo sincronizzatori . .	PORSCHE
rapporti di trasmissione: I	2.256 : 1
II	1.769 : 1
III	1.310 : 1
IV	0.990 : 1
V	0.775 : 1

	RM	2.134 : 1
comando		leva centr.
Differenziale: posizione .		post.
coppia conica . .		ipoide
Rapporto coppia conica		
di serie . . .		1. 4.090 (11/45)
Trasmissione:		
semiassi		a doppi giunti omocinetici
		Lobro

AUTOTELAIO

Telaio: tipo	Tubolare con tubi in acciaio
Sospensioni anteriori: tipo .	a ruote indipendenti con
	bracci a trapezi oscillanti
molle	elicoidali
ammortizzatori . .	2 telescopici idraulici Koni
scuotimento massimo ruote	152 mm
Sospensioni posteriori tipo .	a ruote indipendenti con
	bracci a trapezi oscillanti
molle	elicoidali
ammortizzatori . .	4 telescopici idraulici Koni
scuotimento massimo ruote	150 mm
Stabilizzatori antirollio: tipo	barra di torsione
applicazione . . .	ant. e post.
Ø barre di torsione (ant. post.)	18-16 mm (0.70-0.62 in)
Geometria avantreno:	
convergenza (a carico statico)	
(toe-in)	2 mm (0.76 in)
campanatura (camber) .	0°
inclinazione perno fuso (king-	
pin)	9°
incidenza perno fuso (castor)	5°
Geometria retrotreno:	
convergenza (a carico statico)	
(toe-in)	2-3 mm (0.76-0.78 in)
campanatura (camber) .	—30'
Freni tipo:	a disco Girling autoventilati
comando	idraulico a doppio circuito
	(ant/post) con 1 servofreno
	Girling
diametro dischi ant/post .	267 (10.6 in)
spessori dischi ant/post .	20.6 (0.81 in)
guarnizioni prescritte . .	Ferodo Ferit ID/341
superficie attiva guarnizioni	220 + 220 = 440 cm²
	(68 Sq. in)
Freno di stazionamento: comando	meccanico sulle ruote post.
Sterzo: posizione guida .	sinistra o destra
tipo	cremagliera
diametro sterzata . .	13 m (41.5 ft.)
N. giri volante . . .	3
Ruote: cerchi	lega di magnesio
dimensioni . . .	ant. 7"1/2 JJ x 14"
	Post. 9"1/2 JJ x 14"
Pneumatici: marca e tipo .	Michelin
dimensioni . . .	Ant. 205/70 VR 14 XWX
	Post. 215/70 VR 14 XWX
raggio di rotolamento statico	317 mm (12.5")
Pressioni gonfiaggio:	
ant.	2.5 kg/cm² (35.5 psi)
post.	3 kg/cm² (42.6 psi)

Superimposed on the last page of the factory's specification brochure is the cover of their sales leaflet with once again the comparison being implied between LP 400 and aircraft. It's just a pity that they couldn't have chosen a more suitable jet

Manutenzione periodica

Intervalli sostituzione olio

motore (+ filtro)	5.000 km
cambio	10.000 km
differenziale	10.000 km
scatola guida	

Intervalli ingrassaggio (N ingrassatori

scatola guida	10.000 km
albero di trassione (2)	10.000 km
boccole portamozzo (2)	20.000 km

Sostituzione filtri: olio	5.000 km
aria	20.000 km

CARROZZERIA

Tipo:	Coupé - disegno di Bertone)
N. posti	2

Dimensioni:

lunghezza	4140 mm (163 in)
larghezza	1890 mm (74 in)
altezza	1070 mm (42.2 in)
sbalzo anteriore	910 mm (35.8 in)
sbalzo posteriore	780 mm (30.7 in)
passo	2450 mm (96.5 in)
carreggiata anteriore	1500 mm (58 in)
carreggiata posteriore	1520 mm (60 in)
franco terra	125 mm (4.9 in)
capacità baule	240 lt.

Equipaggiamento:

tergicristallo a velocità regolabile	X

tergicristallo con comando ad intermittenza	X
lavavetro elettrico	X
vetri azzurrati	X
2 x 2 proiettori allo jodio	X
luce retromarcia	X

PESI

PESI	Kg	Lbs.	Rapporto peso pot Kg./Cv	Ripartizione peso ant. % post.	
a secco (con olio e acqua)	1065	2343	2.81	41	59

max ammesso	asse anteriore	Kg. 740 (1630 lb)
	asse posteriore	Kg. 880 (1938 lb)

PRESTAZIONI

Velocità massima	315 Km h (195 mph)
Velocità a 1000 giri in 5ª marcia con coppia conica 1:4,090 (11/45)	29.9 km/h (17,9 mph)
Accelerazione (con due persone) 1 km da fermo	22.8 sec.

RIFORNIMENTI

ORGANI	QUANTITA'		PRODOTTI PRECONIZZATI
Radiatore acqua, motore, riscaldatore	17 lt	29,8 pint 17,9 us qts.	Acqua pura
Serbatoio benzina	120 lt	26,4 Imp. galls 31.5 U.S. galls	Benzina AGIP Supercortemaggiore
Olio motore (coppa + filtro)	15.2 Kg (17.5 lt)	30,6 pint 27,5 U.S. qts.	Olio AGIP Sint 2000 (SAE 20 W - 50)
Ripristino olio motore tra indicazioni • minimo • e • massimo • asticina controllo livello	2,2 kg (2.5 lt)	4,5 pint 2,7 U.S. qts.	Olio AGIP Sint 2000 (SAE 20 W - 50)
Cambio di velocità	3,2 kg (3.65 lt)	6,35 pint 3,82 U.S. qts	Olio AGIP F.1 Rotra SAE 90
Differenziale	4,35 kg (5 lt)	8,7 pints 5,23 U.S. qts.	Olio AGIP F.1 Rotra MP SAE 90
Scatola guida	0,100 kg	0,22 lb.	Olio • HYPOID - SAE 90 •
Liquido freni	0.30 kg (0,345 lt)	6,1 pint 3,61 U.S. qts	CASTROL Girling Brake Fluid Amber oppure AGIP F.1 Brake Fluid Super HD
Serbatoio lavacristallo	1 lt	0,21 imp. galls 0,26 U.S. galls	Acqua pura
Antigelo	> — 10° C < — 0° C > — 14° F < 32° F	3.5 lt.	6 pints 3 us qts	
	> — 15° C < — 10° C > 5° F < 14° F	4 lt.	7 pints 4 us qts	
	> — 20° C < — 15° C > — 4° F < 5° F	5 lt.	8 pints 4.5 us qts	AGIP F.1 Antifreeze
	> — 25° C < — 20° C > — 13° F < — 4° F	5.5 lt.	10 pints 5 us qts	
	> — 30° C < — 25° C > — 22° F < — 13° F	6.5 lt.	11 pints 6 us qts	
	> — 35° C < — 30° C > — 31° F < — 22° F	7 lt.	12 pints 6.5 us qts	

countach

lamborghini

AUTOMOBILI FERRUCCIO LAMBORGHINI S.p.A.

40019 S. AGATA BOLOGNESE (Bologna) - ITALIA - TELEFONI (051) 95.61.71/2/3

CHAPTER SIX

Very low production

Thirty-six months passed between LP 500's show debut and the completion of the first true LP 400 production car. Besides the obvious technical problems, the life of the Countach was and would be continuously disturbed by financial and labour-relations problems. These last cannot be overstressed as reasons for the slowness with which the Countach was put into full production.

In 1974, Rene Leimer, a friend of partner Georges Rossetti, bought Ferruccio Lamborghini's shares and was poised to be the new boss of the factory, Mr Rossetti becoming 'indisposed'. The resultant new confidence brought forth promised sales of 500 V8-engined Urracos per year in the USA and led Stanzani to set a very ambitious production plan for that car. That confidence was destined to end in real disaster. On the other hand, a very much more realistic limited production run of around 50 Countaches per year had been suggested. One year's production was already sold out, and things justifiably looked rosy. In the case of the Countach, there was only one headache—making the cars quickly enough. Imagine the situation Stanzani had to face and understand why he would eventually leave Lamborghini. Constant battles with the unions didn't help either. Little by little the situation was deteriorating. It even led the last Press Officer to tell the authors that 'only very authoritative people [you can see what is meant

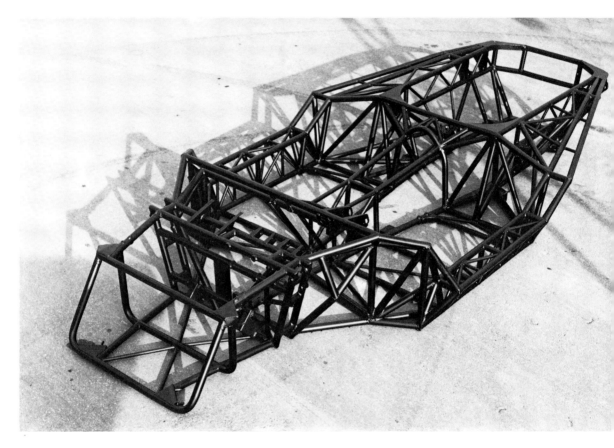

. . .] could do something'. A casual visitor to the works at that time might well have been refused a conducted tour of the assembly shops. Here is a picture of what happened on *Linea Montaggio no. 1.*

'The Countach production line is shaped like an inverted U. When you enter the workshops, you first see the separated door assembly "corner". This is a very important task because of the doors' part in the overall construction of the car and all the elements of adjustment which have to be done most carefully, and because of their sheer size. To gain the courage needed the workers at this station have pinned up pictures of naked women

The chassis in all its glory. Although the tubing is of larger diameter it's complexity of construction would suggest that it too might have taken the Maserati Tipos 60 and 61 nickname of 'Birdcage'. What's not in doubt is its strength

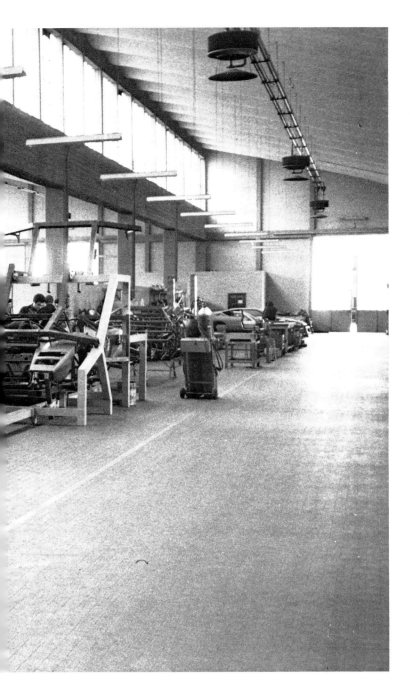

The body assembly line. In the mid background is a bare LP 400 chassis awaiting some panelling, in the middle is the first stage of assembly, chassis in jig, and in the foreground is a bare body/chassis on its hand-pushed way. The factory is both clean and airy

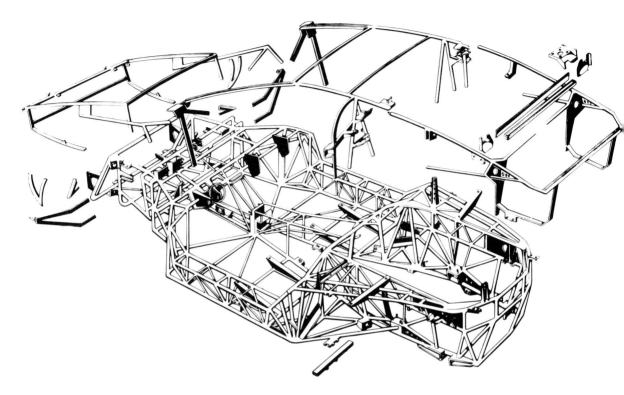

Taken from the parts list, this chassis assembly drawing shows how the bodyshell's individual panels can be attached to the basic frame

all around themselves! The chassis are hand wheeled into the shop past the door assembly unit on small trolleys. Once inside they are to be fitted with the necessary steel structure to make up the skeleton of the body. At the same time, a glass-fibre shell is added to create the floor pan. After that, the chassis is then again hand wheeled to the assembly jig, where all the main structural body panels are welded in. Then the final assembly is ready to be carried out: doors, popping head-lamps, bonnet, etc. . . . The actual finished bodies-cum-chassis are sent to the painting cabin before coming back to the other side of the U line where the mechanical parts are fitted.

'The engines are built on the far side of the

*The first of the line; the
prototype LP 500 in a
genuinely classical setting.*

Above *Three 'doors up'
Countach's out glamourize, if
not outrun, the McDonnell
Douglas F-4 Phantom all-
weather interceptor in the
background*

Right *The first LP 400 at the
factory in its slightly less
than Italian racing red hue.
Note the two wiper arms on
this car*

*A typical Peter Coltrin shot,
for which he is so well known.
Bob Wallace out testing the
first LP 400. The car is not yet
dirty. So maybe he was just
beginning*

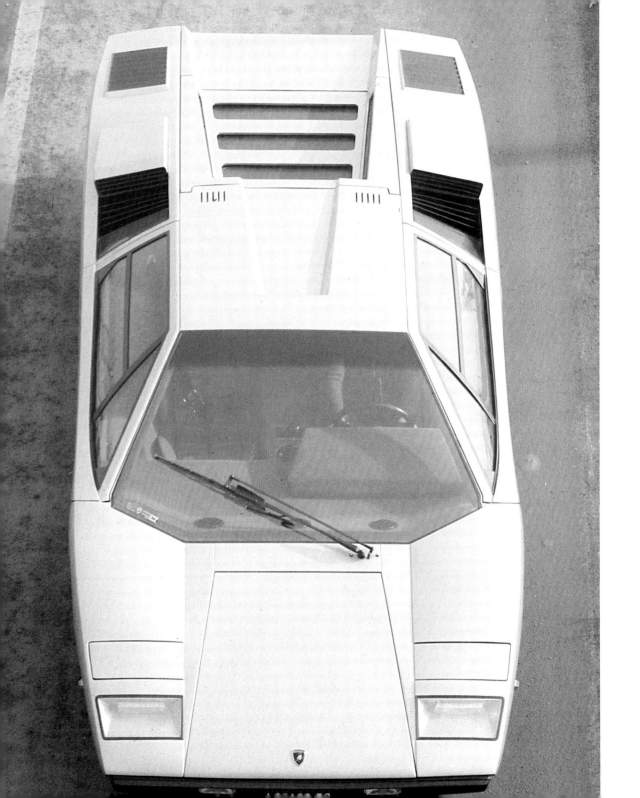

Left *A production LP 400
from above. The wiper arms
of the prototipo have been
changed for a single twin-
blade and driving lamps
have been added to the front
'grille'*

Above *The naked bodyshell
of a Countach S on the hand
moving production line.
There's still considerable
time and money to go before
it is completed*

Far Left *From the front the Countach S is undeniably very striking but from the rear it is perhaps the most aggressive car ever made. Note the Pirelli P7 tyres*

Above *The same Countach S ably displaying its full front spoiler and outset wheel arches to accommodate the wider, restyled wheels and low profile P7s*

Left *Handsome black Lamborghini Countach LP 500 S at rest in the Emilian countryside. Like the fir trees behind it, it's now an evergreen, something unusual for such an exotic car*

Above *Quattrovalvole or four valve. Lamborghini weren't first with exotic car four-valve engines but when it did arrive, no one was disappointed. It is a genuine improvement. External differences between the new car and the previous model are not extensive, however*

Right *The interior improves more gradually. Whatever, those Quattrovalvole seats provide the necessary grip and comfort to driver and passenger alike even if it takes more than a moment to descend into one*

plant, each engine being assembled by one man, much as Aston Martin pride themselves in doing. Engines are hand pushed on a small railway from point to point. Their component parts are mach-

From the previous drawing of the chassis the basic frame is then completed thus. Note the old fashioned trolley on which it sits and is hand pushed along the production line

Further detail body assembly showing the front subframe once tacked onto the basic frame

73

·Here's the door assembly shop with two examples being worked on—they are actually a pair. The doors require very careful assembly because not only must they be extremely strong but also their fit must be very precise. On the wall in the background is their inspiration

ined on the spot (blocks, cylinder heads, crank-shafts, camshafts . . .) after having been cast or forged outside. The test benches are housed separately, at the end of the factory.

'When they come off the line, all the cars are carefully and extensively road tested for both major and last-minute adjustments. Sometimes a car has never come back to the factory, having met a truck or an aggressive Fiat 500.

'A trip with a test driver in a car just off the line

'Inside' the jig for body panel assembly. Three or more men
may work at one station. Once again hand craftsmanship is obvious and necessary

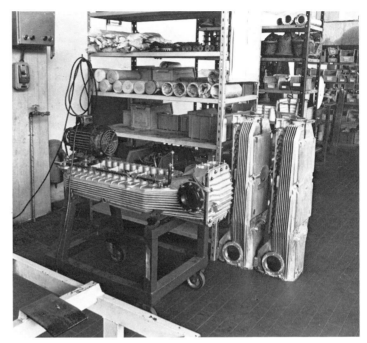

Above left *Crankshaft assembly into the crankcase takes places on this crude but essential jig*

Above right *Testing the transmission shaft in its casing is done before further assembly by powering the shaft with an electric motor*

Right *The LP 400 crankcase and transmission case awaits the two cylinderheads. Note the sunk-in cylinder liners*

Far right above *One cylinderhead awaiting camshafts. The casting quality is beyond criticism*

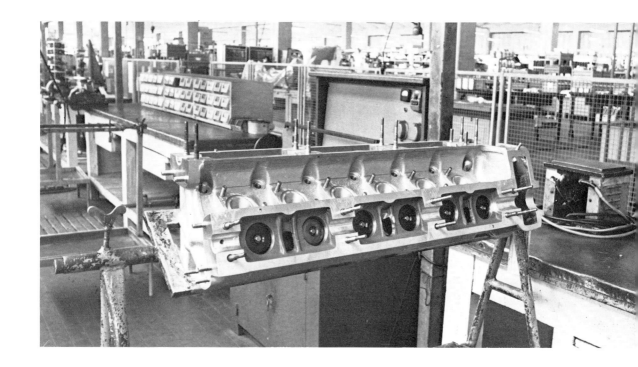

is exceptionally exciting. Our car is orange with
an impressive white leather interior. Stepping
into the beast we notice some minor modifications
brought into the true production version, compared with that green pre-production LP 400. The
front bumper and window frames are finished in
matt black and the side window aperture is a bit
larger, now taking up one-half of the surface area.
Some Lamborghini and Countach badges have
been fitted at the rear of this car and the red frame
around the tail lights is not crossed. There is a
single Bertone emblem without the "B". Inside,
the control lights have been put on the left side of
the driver. Test driver Valentino shows us how to
start the engine and we are surprised by the sound
of a buzzer. This is the transmission oil pump. We

IL PROSSIMO COLLAUDATORE É IL CLIENTE
FATE IN MODO CHE RESTI SODDISFATTO

An LP 400 ready for delivery in November 1975. The slight marks behind the car on the white wall suggest that an over enthusiastic owner may have started the engine too fiercely

have to wait for the oil to warm sufficiently. This buzzing noise will apparently be quietened on the later versions, we are assured.

'Just sitting at the wheel, you feel like you are in the cockpit of a racing car. You see nothing of the front bonnet and your eyes are focused directly on the road. It is almost impossible to look at what is happening at either rear three-quarter angle without outside mirrors. However, the driver position is better than that of the Miura since you are not obliged to fold your legs on each side of the steering wheel. During the first seconds you cannot escape a feeling of claustrophobia, but this soon disappears. At first feel, the gearbox control is precise but not very smooth (should be better on a car which is run-in). The stability and power of the brakes appears to be outstanding and are in accordance with the gasping acceleration. Of course, the suspension settings have been made for very high speed and at 160 km/h (100 mph) or less, you may feel the ride comfort a bit Spartan. The level of engine noise is such to remind you that you are driving a real sports car and is the most attractive music for any enthusiast; it's the most beautiful sound of a savage V12 which can be readily used up to 8000 rpm.

'The only real problem is that the car feels at its best at speeds far over 200 km/h (125 mph) and you do too, but your driving licence does not. The Countach is made for European high-speed cruising. It's not very easy to feel its limits. Naturally, the roadholding of the Countach means understeer, but it tends to be just neutral when you are ready to attack. There is no doubt that the Countach is more effective than the Miura, with better stability at high speed; the nose does not lift. One of the main drawbacks you immediately notice, however, is that the instruments are not easy to read. Facing you, you have a voltmeter,

ammeter, speedometer, oil pressure gauge, water thermometer (coolant), rev counter and fuel level and oil temperature gauges. This is all you need in a true sports car, but at high speed, the diameter of the clocks is too tiny for a quick-glance reading. On the other hand, these instruments seem to be very precise. Our ride was too quick and we did not have time to appreciate the warning lights: brake efficiency, parking light, main beam, alternator, directional lights, hazard warning, hand brake. We have just enough time to dream. A dream that only 23 people afforded in 1974. A happy few. . . .'

A Countach on the street with 'snow tyres'. Note the style of rear light and the occurrence of both 'Lamborghini' and 'Countach' on the rear panel in matt black

CHAPTER SEVEN

The Countach
grows up

Slowly but surely 150 LP 400s were built in the three years between 1974 and 1977 at a production rate well below the potential demand. During these years, factory politics had been very well to the fore. Paolo Stanzani had been replaced by Giampaolo Dallara. In 1975, it was hoped that Walter Wolf would buy the factory and everybody was wooing him most solicitously. There was even talk of a Lamborghini-built Wolf Formula 1 and of a special car for Le Mans. A Formula 1 engine was developed from the Urraco V8, but in the end nothing happened. The factory was still in a very bad way. Rene Leimer applied to Luigi Capellini, ex second-in-command at DeTomaso, to cope with the problems. Capellini tried his very best. He first sought to inject new life into the American market and gave the go-ahead to a new project aimed specifically at the USA; the Silhouette. Only 52 cars, however, were actually built. A contract for the design of a special military four-wheel-drive vehicle, the Cheetah, proved abortive and then there was the equally abortive BMW venture. A lot of money had been spent on the M1 when Munich decided to have their car produced in Germany. Many a sad tale is told of this part of the Lamborghini saga, but this is another story.

Before taking his departure again, G. Dallara spent some time on further development of

Right Countach S. Much has changed for this first LP 500. Apart from the front bumper and spoiler the re-shaped wheel arches and the wheels themselves give clues to its identity

the Countach. His first attempts were carried out
in 1975 on Walter Wolf's personal car, and the
progress made, thanks to the availability of better
tyres, was to benefit the Countach.

Far left above *The smoothness of the original car, the LP 500, has gone. Instead more aggression replaces it but beauty changes as efficiency takes a hold*

Far left *The lightning 'S' and blanket envelopment of the rear wheel arch extensions spell more speed with modern Pirelli P7 tyres*

Above *The Countach S's interior repeats the standard LP 400's*

Left *There were changes to the engine compartment too for the S. Note how the carburettor intakes are trunked off to the scoops, there's much more plumbing to avoid engine emissions*

Nearly finished but not quite. This Countach S needs its doors and other fine fettling before its allowed onto its own wheels and out for extensive road testing. Well illustrated is its most acceptable wheel travel

Today we take the famous Pirelli P7 for granted, with its very low profile and wide section, but at the time it was unknown if the Countach could be made to benefit. Other troubles at the factory, in fact, delayed the introduction of the new version,

but some favoured customers had their cars modified to suit P7 tyres, with new suspension settings and to a lesser extent better brakes. Impressive at first, Countach's brakes proved to be less than effective, according to some owners.

A change in suspension specification for the Countach S shows twin parallel lower links. Note the thickness and diameter of the rear disc, and its obligatory drilled profile. There's no doubting the car's strength and stiffness

It was necessary to wait until the spring of 1978 for the press announcement of the Countach S. There was no increase in engine power, but the chassis came in for a great deal of revision. The front suspension settings were radically altered in order to decrease the large variation of angles in movement. Springs and shock absorbers were given different location points and a new anti-roll bar made the front end more rigid. Different axle bearings (both roller and ball types) were adop-

ted, as well as new aluminium alloy hub carriers. A new steering box was adopted, and the Girling brake calipers were replaced by ATE ones, coupled to ventilated discs of 300 mm diameter. The front 8 1/2 J 15-inch Bravo-style wheels were fitted with 205/50 VR 15 P7 Pirelli tyres.

The rear suspension was also revised. The lower reversed A-arms were replaced with two sets of twin parallel links to eliminate rear axle movement variations caused by tyre deflection

Inside the front compartment of the Countach S there is relatively easy access to the steering rack, brake servo and hydraulic fluid reservoir, washer bottle and the heating and ventilating mechanisms. Presumably that sticker on the car's wing is its build sheet

*Still in bare metal the S
awaits just about everything.
The rows of tyres on the left
hand wall are too narrow for
the Countach. They are for a
series of Brazilian made Fiat
Rusticas being modified
under contract by the factory*

*The front disc of a Countach
S has been beautifully made
and finished. In comparison
the inside of the wheel arch
is perhaps rightly less well
thought of*

when cornering. The rear hub carrier was of a new design, and hub bearings of a larger size. Brake-disc diameter went up to 284 mm at the rear, also with four-piston ATE calipers.

The rear wheels, again of the type first seen on the Bravo, had 12-inch rims and were shod with 345/35 VR 15 P7s.

Two small modifications were made in the

The front spoiler and side extensions, to the wheel arches, are a one piece 'moulding' when fitted to the bodyshell. Work proceeds along the 'S' Linea Montaggio no. 1

This is the Series 2 Countach S interior with a number of style and function improvements although at the last analysis the concept remains much as before. There's a 200 mph speedometer in the left hand large instrument

cockpit. The handbrake lever was relocated on the driver's right-hand side, which is of course, much more practical. The brake mechanism itself was also improved by the use of a special new caliper. The operation of the accelerator pedal was made easier thanks to an upper hinge which allowed the driver's foot to follow it through, avoiding the unpleasant feeling of having one's

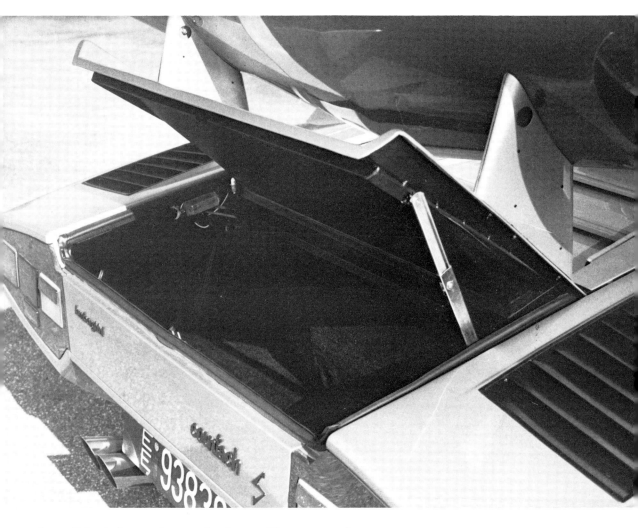

foot lifted from the car's floor. The control was thus more progressive.

Outwardly, the most noticeable changes concerned the body. The wheel arches were enlarged to receive the very squat and wide P7 tyres. These arch or wing extensions were made of glass fibre, as was the front bumper, and were integrated with the chin spoiler and painted in the same colour as

The Series 2 Countach S supports its now famous wing on the rear 'boot lid'. The wing's adjustment facility can be seen through the drilling on the inside support on the left

93

Countach S 2 ready for take-off. From this shot alone it is possible to accept that the style of this car makes it the current, definitive supercar. More obvious now is the door catch in the NACA duct and the small side window just to the rear of the door shut panel. The Bertone 'b' has been lost from above its side name plate as before but Campagnolo can be read on the rear wheel rim

Most expensive pace car in the world? The 1982 Monaco Grand Prix saw this LP 500 S doing service almost as tradition

the body. The wheels were usually finished in silver or gold, but some customers specified such variations as black or even black and white.

For the 1979 Geneva Show, there was a mock-up turbo Countach engine at the request of the new 'owners', the German Hubert Hahn and a Dr. Neumann. The 'simple' turbocharger installation was fitted on the engine in a very amateurish fashion, just for the show, yet it was nothing but another unfulfilled promise from the German team. One has to remember that Hahn had been the West German importer of the marque for some years. The trade court of Bologna which had controlled the factory since 1978 'expelled' the Germans and signed an agreement with the Franco Swiss group Mimran. After having directed the factory on a lease only basis, the Mimran brothers bought it outright in 1980. Patrick Mimran, the young new boss, was going to be responsible for the revival of Lamborghini!

In the meantime, the LP 400 S went on evolving and during the autumn of 1979 the second series, one might call it, appeared. The dashboard was enlarged with bigger instruments including a

Power revival, the LP 500 S was back with 375 quoted horses. Happy Emilian family doesn't own the car but was happy to pose for the photograph. Rest assured they know what the car means to the neighbourhood

dual km/h and mph speedometer afflicted with too many figures that made it difficult to read. The same instrument panel is still used in 1985. The steering wheel's design was not much simpler, using only oval holes. The rear adjustable wing (available only at extra cost) was adopted by many customers. Shortly afterwards, the dihedral wing received a pair of fins and a record production figure was reached in 1980 with a total of 120 Countaches. Giulio Alfieri, called on before as a technical consultant, was appointed chief engineer and plant manager by the Mimran brothers, and he began working seriously on the Countach. The ground clearance of the LP 400 S was increased and new side mirrors were adopted.

However, Lamborghini addicts knew the Countach was missing power. The real power of the LP 400 S had fallen down to about 340/350 hp. The answer came for the 1982 Geneva Show. Thanks to the Alfieri treatment, 375 horses were revived and this at 1000 rpm less than before, together with torque raised to 41.8 mkg at 4500 rpm. To achieve this, the cubic capacity was raised from

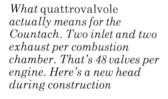

What quattrovalvole actually means for the Countach. Two inlet and two exhaust per combustion chamber. That's 48 valves per engine. Here's a new head during construction

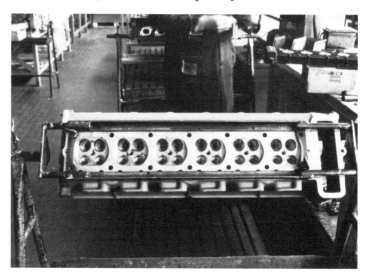

3929 cc to 4754 cc by increasing both bore and stroke: 85.5 × 69 mm instead of 82 × 62 mm. Electronic ignition was adopted and the side-draught carburettors were kept. New transmission ratios were adopted: 1st: 2.232, 2nd: 1.625, 3rd: 1.086, 4th: 0.858 and 5th: 0.707. These are taller ratios, as you can see. The look of the new LP 500 S was unchanged from the LP 400 S, only a 5000 logo at the back made the difference. Lamborghini's revival was illustrated by the strong participation of the Sant'Agata firm in the Monaco Grand Prix where several Countaches were used as pace cars. Another detail modification could be noticed on these and the next production Coun-

Major distinguishing external changes for the Quattrovalvole, apart from the badge itself, is the remodelled engine cover clearly shown here

99

taches: the wheels were no longer manufactured by Campagnolo but by OZ.

When I then asked Giulio Alfieri about four-valve engines, he answered that he felt it a useless modification for the Countach. This was partly true. At the 1985 Geneva Show, Lamborghini answered the new Ferrari Testarossa with the Countach Quattrovalvole. Alfieri told me shortly afterwards that it was sometimes necessary to adapt one's opinion to the needs of the firm you are working for, and the marketplace. In addition, four-valve heads could bring more power in a 'safer' way than turbocharging could do. Once again, Alfieri modified a lot of the V12, keeping only the original block castings. Pistons, rods, liners, crankshaft were new.

This time the cubic capacity was raised to 5167 cc by adding 6 mm to the stroke. The most striking alteration, of course, was the completely new four-valve heads with pentagonal combustion chambers. Two inlet valves of 36 mm diameter replaced one valve of 48 mm and two exhaust valves of 32 mm took the place of one valve of 38.2 mm. The reputed 'bad breathing' of the Countach engine caused by side draught carburettors was stopped finally by adopting vertical downdraught 44 DCNF Webers. This ended in a maximum torque of 51.5 mkg DIN at 5200 rpm, little better than the Testarossa. The power jumped to 455 hp DIN at 7000 rpm, really much better than the Ferrari Testarossa which only has 390 hp, and that was not all. Alfieri also decided to put an end to the hard and slow operating gearbox by adopting a new ZF synchromesh system although, in fact, early Quattrovalvole Countaches still have the Porsche synchromeshed transmission.

Once again, the look of the car is virtually unchanged. In order to accommodate the vertical

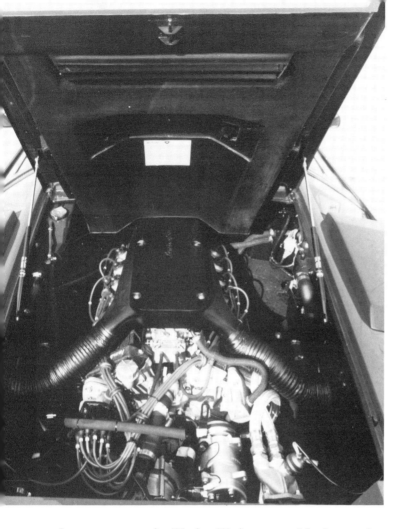

Reason for the raised engine cover is the taller air cleaner box necessitated by the new downdraught Weber carburettors. Electronic ignition complicates matters, too

carburettors, a 'millefeuille' was added on the engine cover. One detail worth mentioning is the first time use of Kevlar for the front and rear lids. Of course, there is a Quattrovalvole logo added to the tail of the car. Between 1980 and 1985, the body of the Countach has remained the same. Alfieri preferred to concentrate on reliability, finish and quality of production. Minor modifications were apparent in the cockpit with an altered central console and glove box cover and leather-padded window cranks.

CHAPTER EIGHT

Making it more exclusive

Above right Complete with lots of road dirt, a sill dent and an oil stain on the front wheel Walter Wolf's first Countach returns from testing. Note the Bologna Prova plate and the special rear compartment clips

Right The first Wolf car was a modified LP 400 painted red fitted with his 'own' 5 litre engine, tacked-on wheel arches, black wing and Bravo wheels with P7s. It's not, therefore, a prototype S but it must have been an influence. Wolf's front wheel arches were not the right shape to avoid grit from blasting the paint off the rear extensions

Owning one of the rarest and most impressive cars in the world is not enough for a certain class of customer who does not wish to have even the same car as any other mortal; it would, for instance, be terrible to have an identical car to anyone else at the Monaco Grand Prix!

It is not very easy to trace all the custom variations on the Countach theme, many of them having been made outside the factory, in Japan, the USA or Germany. The best-known cars of this special breed are those made for Walter Wolf. After his standard white LP 400, the Austro-Canadian magnate had three special versions prepared for him. These cars were developed by Dallara personally during his second stay at Lamborghini. All Wolf's cars have been fitted with but one single 5-litre engine (the second built by the factory), which remains Lamborghini property and is removed every time Mr Wolf changes his car. The first version was built in 1975. Painted in red, it had black wing extensions and for the first time the now well-known fully adjustable rear wing was fitted. The Bravo-style wheels were fitted with P7s, as on the current S version. The car had his own 'Personal' Formula 1 steering wheel fitted and racing fire extinguisher. The chin spoiler and front wing extension were not

Above *Walter Wolf's second car, this time painted blue, was built in 1976 although this photograph was taken later in Germany. What aren't obvious from this shot are the 'gold' wheels and mirrors, coachlines and a public address system! It's still a modified LP 400 not an S*

Right *Walter Wolf, with the loose tie, with Giampaolo Dallara (his height) to his right, and others, pose before his hidden first modified, red LP 400 at the factory*

of the same shape as those of the Countach S. Wolf's red car was called the LP 500S.

A second, very similar version was built the following year. This one was finished in a light marine blue and decorated with gold strips and Wolf emblems. The rear wing was electrically adjustable from the cockpit and Wolf could speak directly to other motorists via a public address system! While his first custom, the red car, was sent to Japan, where it is said to have burnt out, this second now belongs to a happy German fanatic.

The third and latest car commissioned by Wolf

Countach 5000SS—an American modified shows much work yet hides a 5 litre engine, may be?

was a modified S. This car was the first Countach S produced by the factory, but it was far from being a standard example. The same 5-litre engine was again installed, but this time the brakes had eight pistons per caliper (specially designed by Automotive Products). The clutch was Borg & Beck double-disc type. The steering was more direct and the front-to-rear balance of the brakes

was adjustable from the driver's seat. The car was painted in the Wolf racing colours of very dark blue and gold, and was even fitted with Wolf badges on the wheels. This car, it seems, is still owned by Walter Wolf. (However, in the author's opinion, the most incredible custom version made at the Sant'Agata plant was for a famous customer in Haiti. This Wolf-style car was blue and

The same 5000SS shows strange work on the side lights and strong polish on the front wheels

The front of the blue and gold Wolf-style car still at the factory. Paint overkill perhaps spoils this idea although as a head-turner no one can deny its success

gold, with matching interior, with even many parts of the engine finished in gold as well!)

Besides these factory versions, some other customers have made their own modifications, mostly fitting wide wheel arches for even wider rims. The so-called 5000SS in America is home-modified; the 5-litre engine is not to original factory specification.

The only known open Countach was made by Lolita Automobile Development in Australia. This was a modified LP 400 à la Wolf with its roof simply cut off as though by a tin opener. This car was once used for an acceleration contest with a Mirage IIID jet. On the standing 400-metre sprint, the aircraft took 10.8 seconds and the Countach 12.7 after leading for the first 300 metres.

Even the interior was gold and dark blue. Lucky the man who should have to match the gold leather of the interior with the gold gloss on the bodyshell and the alloy of the road wheels! Mr Silvera of Haiti apparently left the ignition key in cheap chrome

Above left *Koenig's Countach follows his familiar Ferrari style with general smoothing of rear wing and side 'skirts'. No one will actually say it improves the original*

Above right *Twin turbo Countach. More is just more. Neat conversion by Albert but the factory went to four valves instead, at least, this time*

Below left *More of the same. Obviously there are at least two such 'custom' Countaches in existence. In fact, there are many more but none so well done as this particular one*

Below right *Turbo boost gauge and stringback gloves. Both essential for turbo Countach*

However, the Countach has become a more common car with time: ten years after its launch it has reached a total production figure a little superior to that of the Miura. Falling into many more hands, it could not escape the custom mania: there have been revamped interiors, pink bodywork, side steps and so on. In Germany, the famous Ferrari 'specialist' Willy Koening marketed a special exhaust for the Countach (and claimed to bring more power) plus side steps, a special rear wing similar to the one sold for Ferraris, and a pair of front spacers to widen the track.

Two special engines must also be quoted, both are in LP 400 S models. In Switzerland, Lambo fanatic Max Bobnar had his car fitted with a pair of turbochargers by the Austrian tuning expert Albert. Perhaps less dramatic, a Luxembourger engineeer put vertical Miura carburettors on his LP 400 S.

Custom bodywork and twin turbo engine means expense. No performance figures are published

Above *The turbo Countach must make a superb noise with the traditional four-cam growl supplemented by the whine of the turbines' rotors*

Right *New engine cover for a Countach now fitted with Miura downdraught carburettors. An ironic presumption before the 5000 Quattrovalvole which also has finished with the side-draught versions*

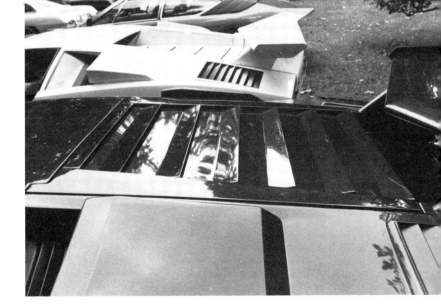

CHAPTER NINE

Making it legal
for the USA

When he conceived the Countach, Stanzani did
not consider its sale on the American market and
he did not do so on purpose. In view of the
problems encountered by the Miura towards the
end of its production life, it was apparent that
making the Countach street-legal in the USA
would have cost a lot more than the factory could
afford. Further, sales would not have justified the
additional expenses. This, however, never pre-
vented people from importing these cars and there
are now far more Countaches in the USA than in
England or France. These cars are used mainly
for shows and are, therefore, not street-legal, nor
have they been homologated individually. Some
companies specialize in the 'legalization' of exotic
cars and are now used to converting Countaches.
These firms offer various types of conversion. It
seems incredible, but not one US-legalized Countach looks like another; some are very close to the
European version and have almost no exterior
differences (how was the 5 mph impact bumper
problem with these cars solved?), the others look
horrible. One of the ugliest versions is the
experimental car made with the assistance of the
factory and commissioned by Sheldon Brooks of
Minnesota. This Countach is just not beautiful,
having been adapted to meet the local regulations
with a total disregard for elegance. Many months

of work were needed to meet the demands for sustaining 10 mph frontal and 5 mph rear-end impact. All the structure had to be reinforced. Stronger frame members were fitted fore and aft of the passenger pod, and guard beams in the doors. Among the obvious additions are the huge front bumper and the modified chin spoiler with additional air inlets. The rear end was less ugly but very strong. The tail lights were bigger, Ferrari

Making the Countach S American street-legal was difficult but the factory managed it without bastardizing its profile too much. That front bumper and the inset side lights can have done nothing for its aerodynamics but then at 55 mph . . .

115

The rear of the US-specification S shows off an emissions controlled exhaust system, round rear lamps, inset side marker lights, another look at the registration plate illuminator and an impact conscious rear 'dam' for a bumper

style, and wheel arches were in aluminium and not glass fibre.

One of the most interesting aspects of the car was its engine, being overbored to 4.4 litres. It is said to give 473 bhp on the bench. Of course, this was before the EPA exhaust emissions modifications. This made it the most powerful US legal Countach. However, its look was not very attractive.

With the arrival of Alfieri, Lamborghini decided to tackle the US market with more efficiency and this had to begin with a good US legal version of the Countach. It led to a Bosch fuel-injected version of the LP 500 S producing 330 hp at 6000 rpm and 44 mkg at 5000 rpm. This car was homologated with a modified nose and tail, and this time the US Countach has a better look, with nicely integrated crash deformable ends.

Legal too in the USA. This is the factory fresh US version. Note side marker and special rear bumper

CHAPTER TEN

Conclusion

Lamborghini is now on the right way and according to Ingegnere Alfieri, 'the future of the Countach is in the hands of God'. Frankly speaking, the Countach is well alive and will live more years with more improvements. Sometime around 1986, a new revamped version is awaited. The new car will have an altogether bigger and wider rear section with wide air inlets for the radiators. The airboxes will be suppressed and side steps will be added under the doors. The front end treatment should be lightened.

Production figures		
1974:	23	
1975:	60	LP 400
1976:	27	
1977:	40	
1978:	16	
1979:	40	LP 400 S
1980:	120	
1981:	88	
1982:	96	LP 500 S
1983:	114	
1984:	132	
Total LP 400 = 150		
Total LP 400 S = 385		
Total LP 500 S = 325		

Road & Track, February 1976: The fastest car we've ever tested

Reprinted in full with kind permission from *Road & Track* **magazine, issue dated February 1976.**

Those who decried man's journeys to the moon as flights of madness need not read further, because the same kind of dedication, blind enthusiasm and technical advancement that led to those initial space triumphs is seen in the Lamborghini Countach.

If you don't love cars, don't even try to understand the Countach. Its no-holds-barred, cost-no-object design is, on one hand, one of extremes and excesses and, on the other, a mobile demonstration representing the pinnacle of automotive design, technical achievement and sophistication, the likes of which we will probably never again see. We can think of few cars that are endowed with the emotional and visual charisma of the Countach. Its brutally angular Bertone body is striking from every angle. It has enough NACA ducts, scoops and vents to keep an aerodynamicist content for a lifetime. Its upward-tilting doors carefully counterweighted on assisting hydraulic struts are a designer's delight. But more than all those things the Countach is an extremely well engineered car that has evolved from an idea car at Geneva in 1971 to a production car two years later. Many thought such a transition impossible, citing the Countach's aerospace-style body and its midship design with a longitudinal engine, a gearbox *ahead* of the engine and power takeoff running *back* through the engine sump to a ZF limited-slip differential as impractical for a road car. But Lamborghini proved all his detractors wrong and is currently producing Countachs at the rate of about one a week.

At the moment the Countach is not certified for sale in the U.S. so the example we tested came to us via the extremely good graces of Steve Milne of Vancouver, British Columbia.

The Countach is not totally foreign to the R & T staff. Our man in Italy, Pete Coltrin, wrote a technical analysis of the car in November 1973 and two-and-a-half years later (R & T June 1975) our newest staff member at the time, Tom Bryant, was the envy of the rest of the R & T staff when he was offered a ride in a Countach from Los Angeles to Phoenix by Dan Morgan, President of the U.S. importer for Lamborghini.

Reading about a car is one thing. Seeing it in the flesh, driving it and testing it is an entirely different matter. We sometimes

Production—the standard 'off the shelf' LP 400

approach cars like the Countach with trepidation, fearing that it won't live up to our expectations. With the Countach we worried for naught. Just a few minutes behind the wheel was enough to convince every driver that the Countach delivered everything it promised and more. Open the door, slide in (climb would probably be a more appropriate term as the door sills are very wide . . . and don't forget to duck your head) and you slip into a very comfortable body-hugging seat (being thin is a distinct advantage). There are no seat adjustments other than for fore-and-aft location but the curvature of the one-piece bucket is ideal and the contours hold you tightly in place when the car is cornering hard. Combine this with a steering wheel adjustable for reach and height and you come up with a driving position that will suit almost any driver up to 5 ft 10 in. tall. The footwells are narrow but there's plenty of leg and elbow room and the large dead pedal is most appreciated.

Interior appointments are what you'd expect of a $52,000 car: first rate. Leather covers the seats, console and door-trim panels while the usual Italian suede-like velour completely covers the dash and the huge shelf under the sharply raked windshield. A full complement of Stewart-Warner gauges—well placed for easy viewing—is directly in front of the driver. Here we'd like to register a mild complaint. The instruments are covered with flat glass and during the day stray reflections sometimes make the gauges difficult to read.

Two stalks—one on each side of the steering column—incorporate the horn, turn signals and high beams (left) and wiper and washer functions (right). The pop-up headlights operate electrically from a rocker switch on the console directly in front of the shift lever.

There's a surprising amount of luggage room in a deep square box behind the engine compartment. Fill this and you can still squeeze a few small items up front with the spare tire or behind the seats if they aren't pushed full back.

Being seen in a Countach is a real ego trip; but seeing out is another story. The view directly in front or to the rear is fine. The sharply sloping front fenders aren't well defined so one must park with caution, but that's the least of your problems. Rear quartering vision is for all intents and purposes nonexistent. The small convex fender mirrors have to be adjusted precisely to afford the driver even minimal coverage on his flanks. Driving the Countach in traffic, especially at night is intimidating, to say the least. Lesser cars hover around it like drones around a queen bee and you can never be sure when some other driver will dive in for a closer look. All this has to be a bit worrisome to the Countach owner who knows that his aluminum body panels are only one millimeter thick and that even errant hand pressure will dimple the body work. Poking one's head out the side window to check traffic is not recommended either because the Countach's windows roll down only about three inches!

Although the first prototype Countach was fitted with a 5-litre V-12, all production Countachs have a four-cam 3929-cc V-12 that differs only slightly from the one used to power the Miura. What a treat to sample the response of the Countach's relatively uncontrolled engine. We have become so accustomed to low compression ratios, retarded timing, exhaust-gas recirculation, surging, stumbling and like problems that we sometimes forget how it was in the good old days BS (Before Smog). Pump the throttle once and the engine lights instantly, hot or cold. Turn it off and it stops right now, no run-on, no backfiring. Driveability was nearly perfect except for a distinct tendency for the engine to foul plugs in prolonged city driving. But the engine responded well to an 'Italian tuneup'—a few quick bursts up near the 8000 rpm redline and the V-12 was in fine fettle again. With six big Webers keeping the engine healthy and happy it's no surprise that the V-12 likes revs. Nail the throttle below 4000 rpm and the engine takes on a totally different character developing the V-12 wail that's music to an enthusiast's ears and surging toward the redline with no detectable drop-off in power. We didn't find a road where we could really let the Countach stretch its legs; our usual top speed section got very short very quickly. But we saw 7000 rpm in 5th gear for an instant and the engine was still pulling so strongly that we don't question its ability to pull 8000 rpm (192 mph) in top gear. A standing quarter mile in 14.4 sec at 105.5 mph and a 0–60 mph time of 6.8 sec are most impressive for a car weighing 3020 lb but these times and speeds were achieved without the benefit of the wheelspinning starts that can cut valuable seconds off acceleration times. The fat Michelin XWX radials are very sticky and the clutch, though perfectly adequate, wasn't designed for drag racing starts. Our English cousins at *Motor* recently tested a Countach and by suppressing their feelings of mechanical sympathy, winding the engine up to 7000 rpm and releasing the clutch as sharply as possible achieved some spectacular results, including two black lines 50 yards long, a 0–60 mph time of 5.6 sec and a quarter-mile time of 14.1 sec. In deference to the almost irreplaceable nature of the car (and to the owner who was standing near by) we opted for a less auspicious and safer technique: namely driving the car away from the line smoothly and punching the throttle as the revs neared 4000 rpm. With proper traction (more precisely less of it) the Countach should be capable of tripping the quarter-mile lights in the high 12s or low 13s.

The forward mounting of the gearbox is a particularly neat solution for a mid-engine road car as it obviates the usual long shift linkage and provides a direct positive gear change. The Countach is without a doubt one of the best shifting of the mid-engine exoticars. Shift effort is high but the synchros are unbeatable and shifts are fast and precise despite the implications of an external metal gate to guide the lever.

The Countach has exemplary road manners. Another advantage Lamborghini engineers cite for positioning the V-12 engine for-and-aft with the gearbox ahead of the engine is weight distribution. They claim and our testing proved that the longitudinal layout gives better directional stability than the Miura's because the big mass is closer to the center of gravity and the aerodynamic pressure center. The Countach's superb air-cutting shape enters into this too, and we can't remember testing another car that felt more stable at speed—above 130 mph and on any road surface—than the Countach. Equally and perhaps even more important than straight-line stability is cornering. Here too the Countach excels. The Countach is an extremely well balanced car with none of the abrupt trailing throttle oversteer that characterizes some mid-engine exoticars. Back off when cornering hard and the tail comes out smoothly, gently and controllably; keep applying

power and the nose drifts toward the outside of the curve ever so slightly. The steering is quick and precise at all speeds with effort decreasing from moderate to just right with increasing road speed. There's excellent road feel and transitional response, minimal kickback from the steering on bumpy surfaces and the Michelin tires give a firm grip when cornering (but not much warning as their limit is reached) allowing the Countach to be placed with great accuracy. Despite the lowness of the car (it's only 42.1 in. tall) there's a surprising amount of wheel travel—over 3.5 in. up front and nearly 6 in. at the rear—so while the ride is firm it's comfortably supple and well controlled, not harsh or jerky. That wheel travel also means the Countach traverses dips and bumps with surprising aplomb. The

Comparison—production LP 400 with 2·4 litri single cam Urraco engine through the window

brakes—big ventilated discs all around—performed impressively in our tests, stopping the Countach in very short distances and with excellent control. As expected the brakes exhibited no fade and although the pedal only requires 18 lb for a $\frac{1}{2}$g stop it is easy to modulate smoothly when slowing the Countach from very high speeds.

Very few cars regardless of price provide the spine-tingling thrills and excitement that driving a Countach provokes. Is the Countach the ultimate exoticar? Probably. Is it a perfect car? No. No car is flawless and as we said before the rear quarter vision is poor. But worst of all, the seatbelts are lousy!

ROAD TEST
LAMBORGHINI COUNTACH

SCALE: 10" DIVISIONS

PRICE

List price .... approx $52,000
Price as tested ..... approx $52,000
　　Price as tested includes standard
　　equipment (air conditioning,
　　AM/FM/tape deck)

MANUFACTURER

Automobili Ferruccio Lamborghini
　Spa
40019 Sant'Agata Bolognese
Bologna, Italy

GENERAL

Curb weight, lb	3020
Test weight	3230
Weight distribution (with driver), front/rear, %	43/57
Wheelbase, in.	96.5
Track, front/rear	59.1/59.8
Length	163.0
Width	74.4
Height	42.1
Ground clearance	4.9
Overhang, front/rear	36.7/29.8
Usable trunk space, cu ft	7.5
Fuel capacity, U.S. gal.	31.7

ENGINE

Type	dohc V-12
Bore x stroke, mm	82.0 x 62.0
Equivalent in.	3.23 x 2.44
Displacement, cc/cu in.	3929/240
Compression ratio	10.5:1
Bhp @ rpm, DIN	375 @ 8000
Equivalent mph	192
Torque @ rpm, DIN, lb-ft	266 @ 5000
Carburetion	six Weber 45 DCOE (2V)
Fuel requirement	premium, 98-oct

DRIVETRAIN

Transmission	5-sp manual
Gear ratios: 5th (0.78)	3.19:1
4th (0.99)	4.05:1
3rd (1.31)	5.36:1
2nd (1.77)	7.24:1
1st (2.26)	9.24:1
Final drive ratio	4.09:1

ACCOMMODATION

Seating capacity, persons	2
Seat width	2 x 14.0
Head room	34.5
Seat back adjustment, deg	0

CHASSIS & BODY

Layout .... mid engine/rear drive
Body/frame .... tubular steel
　chassis/aluminum panels
Brake system .. 10.5-in. vented discs
　front and rear, vacuum assisted
　Swept area, sq in. 416
Wheels ...... Campagnolo cast alloy;
　14 x 7½JJ front, 14 x 9JJ rear
Tires .... Michelin XWX;
　205/70VR-14 f, 215/70VR-14 r
Steering type .... rack & pinion
　Turns, lock-to-lock 3.0
　Turning circle, ft 42.7
Front suspension: unequal-length
　A-arms, coil springs, tube shocks,
　anti-roll bar
Rear suspension: upper lateral links,
　lower reversed A-arms, upper &
　lower trailing arms, dual coil
　springs, dual shock absorbers,
　anti-roll bar

INSTRUMENTATION

Instruments: 320-km/h speedo,
　9000-rpm tach, 99,999.9 odo, oil
　press., oil temp, coolant temp,
　ammeter, voltmeter, fuel level
Warning lights: brake sys, hand
　brake, alternator, a/c fan, a/c
　compressor, hazard, parking
　lights, high beam, directionals

MAINTENANCE

Service intervals, mi:
Oil change	3000
Filter change	3000
Chassis lube	6000
Minor tuneup	3000
Major tuneup	6000
Warranty, mo/mi	6/6000

CALCULATED DATA

Lb/bhp (test weight)	8.6
Mph/1000 rpm (5th gear)	23.3
Engine revs/mi (60 mph)	2570
Piston travel, ft/mi	1045
R&T steering index	1.28
Brake swept area, sq in./ton	258

Road & Track's ever consistant
specifications table

ROAD TEST
RESULTS

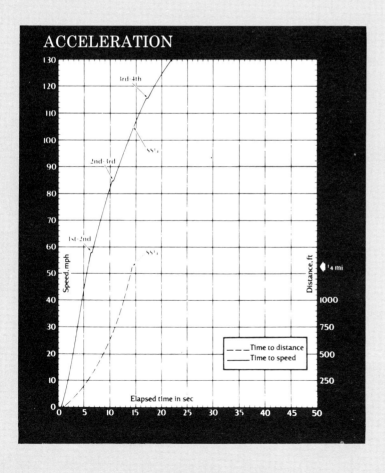

ACCELERATION

ACCELERATION
Time to distance, sec:
0-100 ft	3.2
0-500 ft	8.1
0-1320 ft (¼ mi)	14.6
Speed at end of ¼ mi, mph	100.5

Time to speed, sec:
0-30 mph	2.6
0-50 mph	4.6
0-60 mph	5.9
0-70 mph	7.7
0-100 mph	14.4
0-110 mph	17.7

SPEEDS IN GEARS
5th gear (7500 rpm)	est 164
4th (8000)	140
3rd (8000)	108
2nd (8000)	81
1st (8000)	64

FUEL ECONOMY
Normal driving, mpg	11.0
Cruising range, mi (1-gal. res)	338

HANDLING
Speed on 100-ft radius, mph	35.7
Lateral acceleration, g	0.852
Speed thru 700-ft slalom, mph	63.6

BRAKES
Minimum stopping distances, ft:
From 60 mph	131
From 80 mph	226
Control in panic stop	excellent
Pedal effort for 0.5g stop, lb	15

Fade: percent increase in pedal effort to maintain 0.5g deceleration
in 6 stops from 60 mph	nil
Parking: hold 30% grade?	no
Overall brake rating	excellent

INTERIOR NOISE
All noise readings in dBA:
Idle in neutral	74
Maximum, 1st gear	102
Constant 30 mph	82
50 mph	85
70 mph	85
90 mph	88

SPEEDOMETER ERROR
60 km/h (37.3 mph)	
indicated is actually	43.0
80 km/h (49.7 mph)	54.0
100 km/h (62.1 mph)	71.5
120 km/h (74.6 mph)	86.0
140 km/h (87.0 mph)	100.0

Road & Track, December 1978: Still the ultimate exotic?

Reprinted in full with kind permission from *Road & Track* **magazine issue dated December 1978.**

The last two times we've compiled lists of the Ten Best Cars in the world (June 1975 and 1978), the Lamborghini Countach hasn't been included, but it has been given special recognition each time as the most exotic car in the world, and deservedly so. That's a rather significant achievement considering the original Bertone concept car debuted as the Geneva auto show in 1971 and made the transition to a production car in 1973. Five years later, it remains a singularly outstanding example of Lamborghini's commitment to building an unrivaled automotive masterpiece. We road tested the Countach in February 1976 and found it to be the fastest production car we'd ever tested with a 0–100 mph time of 13.3 seconds and a top speed of 192 mph. Incredible. In 1977, Lamborghini made some revisions to the car and designated the new model the Countach S. When Dan Morgan of Automotive Compliance Inc, the engineering division of American Specialty Corp (25518 Frampton Ave, Harbor City, Calif. 90710; 213 539–4880), a firm that qualifies imported cars to meet U.S. safety and emissions standards, offered us the opportunity to test the S in U.S.-legal trim, we eagerly accepted.

Before we get into the actual road test of the S, let's review the basics of the car's design. It's quite clear that Lamborghini set out to make the Countach the ultimate mid-engine sports car, so the initial step was a tubular space-frame chassis with a 1.0-mm thick aluminum body laid over it. Exotic aircraft materials go into the chassis to keep weight to a minimum and thus maximize handling and performance. The aluminum body is an exotic car fancier's dream come true—angular, unique, beautifully ugly from some angles but always beautiful in overall appearance; a car that provokes response from everyone who notices it, man or woman, adult or child.

What sets the Countach S apart from the original version primarily are larger and wider wheels and different tires. The S uses Campagnolo cast alloy $15 \times 8\frac{1}{2}$ wheels front and 15×12 rear, versus $14 \times 7\frac{1}{2}$ front and 14×9 rear on the previous model. The new wheels are designed to accept Pirelli P7 radial tires that measure 205/50VR-15 up front and 345/35VR-15 at the rear— replacing the Michelin XWX radials (205/70VR-14 front, 215/70VR-14 rear) of earlier cars and giving the Countach a remarkable amount of rubber contact with the road. The new wheels and tires necessitated fender flares. The front flares carry forward to merge into a chin spoiler, while the rear flares travel back and beneath the upswept tail, almost like small mudguards. We had a strong difference of opinion on the esthetic effects of the flares, with some staffers feeling they finish the car off nicely and somewhat soften the bullet shape of the car, while others opined that they look tacked on and upset the aerodynamic and crisp lines of the original design.

The basic design of the Countach's suspension is unchanged, consisting of unequal-length A-arms, coil springs, tube shocks and an anti-roll bar in the front; at the rear, upper lateral links, lower reversed A-arms, upper and lower trailing arms, dual coil springs, dual tube shocks and an anti-roll bar handle the chores. Because of the wheel and tire change, however, the suspension geometry has been altered. The Pirelli P7 tires need to run as flat and straight as possible for optimum effectiveness so the toe-in is set at zero degrees and camber change has been reduced to a minimum.

The combination of suspension and tires produces handling that can only be described as superb, with limits so high they are virtually impossible to reach under normal circumstances. The rack-and-

Aggression—the preying 'mantis'—first Countach S

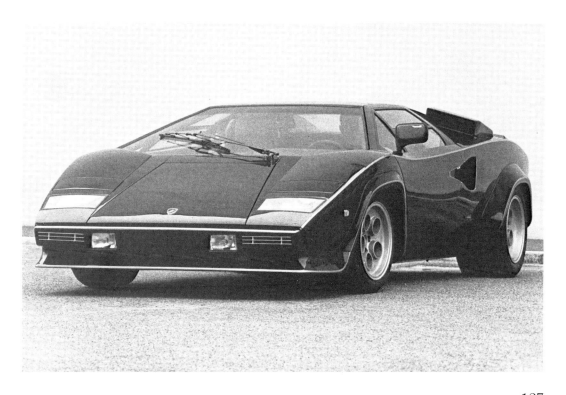

That first Countach S—function/style

pinion steering and the ventilated disc brakes at all four wheels are also excellent, and the Countach S is confidence inspiring as it tracks through fast bends with an uncanny grace that surpasses the courage of most drivers to press it as hard as it will go. The Pirelli P7 tires are much more forgiving than the previous Michelins, which give little warning as their limit approaches. On the skidpad and in our slalom test, we found the Countach S an impressive car in transitions and an easy car to control in steady-state cornering. There is mild understeer on the skidpad when power is applied; back off and the tail comes out, but very slowly and in an easy-to-control manner that never poses a threat. It's interesting to note that it tied the Ferrari 308 GTB for best skidpad performance, and the 1977 Corvette for best slalom speed of any production car we've tested.

In high-speed driving, the Countach S is exemplary up to 130 mph, with an eerie stability that belies speeds of 100 plus. Above 130 mph, however, we found it to be less than ideal, with a tendency to wander about on the road as the front end seemed to lighten; something we hadn't noted with the previous Countach. Morgan, on the other hand, says he has found the S more stable than earlier cars during sustained periods of high-speed (130 mph plus) driving in Europe.

The ride characteristics are very much what you'd expect from a car of this type: firm but compliant and not upsetting to either occupants or the car's stability. There is virtually no body roll on even the sharpest, fastest corners, and all in all it feels like you're driving a very good race car.

And what of the drivetrain that supplies the power for all this driving pleasure? The Countach S engine is a slightly detuned version of the traditional Countach 4-cam 4-liter V-12. The normal Countach engine (which actually dates back to Lamborghini's famed Miura of the Sixties) develops 375 bhp DIN at 8000 rpm and 266 lb-ft torque at 5000 from its 3929-cc capacity. The S version, however, is rated at 353 bhp DIN at 7500 rpm (torque is 267 lb-ft at 5500), primarily because of different carburation (still using six side-draft Webers but of smaller size). ACI estimates the V-12 in U.S.-legal configuration develops 325 bhp.

The Countach's mid-engine design is unique in that the V-12 engine is mounted longitudinally and the gearbox is ahead of the engine—as a result, unlike other mid-engine cars, this Lamborghini has virtually direct shift linkage. the gearbox is a 5-speed and both 4th and 5th gears are overdrive ratios (0.99 and 0.76:1, respectively) for long-legged cruising, while the final drive ratio is a low 4.09:1 for quick acceleration.

The performance of the S, despite the drop in bhp and the addition of emission controls (dual catalytic converters, thermal reactors and airinjection pumps along with massive amounts of heat shielding material) designed by ACI's chief engineer, Jas Rarewala, is damned impressive: 0–60 mph in 5.9 sec, 0–80 in less than 10.0 sec, and 0–100 mph in 14.4 sec. The standing-start quarter mile was covered in 14.6 sec at a terminal velocity of 100.5 mph. Quick enough!

Under heavy throttle below 3000 rpm the engine had a tendency to stumble, but once it smoothed out the tach needle raced to the 8000-rpm redline and gave the feeling the engine would gladly continue to 10,000 rpm if the driver permitted. And the sound—noisy, but with that magical, musical noise that only a V-12 can make. The Automotive Compliance Inc emission system installation is expertly done and the engine fires up with just a few cranks of the starter motor. It's also gratifying to note that there was no tendency toward overheating despite the add-on emission controls. Those controls do take their toll on the top end, however, and our estimate is that the Countach S in desmogged trim would top out at 7500 rpm in 5th gear, which translates to *only* 164 mph, compared to 175 mph for the S without emission controls. Oh well, clean air is important too.

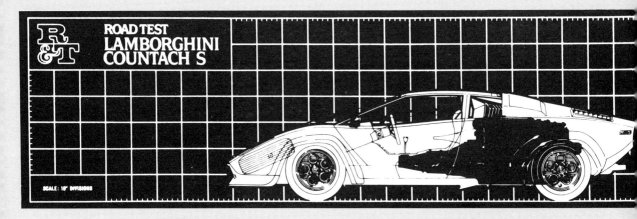

ROAD TEST
LAMBORGHINI COUNTACH S

SCALE: 10" DIVISIONS

PRICE

List price .... built to special order only
Price as tested $85,000
   Price as tested includes: air
   freight (approx $5000), safety &
   emissions qualification (approx
   $17,000)

REMANUFACTURER

American Specialty Corp
25518 Frampton Ave
Harbor City, Calif. 90710

GENERAL

Curb weight, lb	3170
Test weight	3250
Weight distribution (with driver), front/rear, %	42/58
Wheelbase, in.	96.5
Track, front/rear	58.7/64.3
Length	163.0
Width	78.7
Height	42.1
Ground clearance	4.9
Overhang, front/rear	36.7/29.8
Usable trunk space, cu ft	2.7
Fuel capacity, U.S. gal.	31.7

ENGINE

Type	dohc V-12
Bore x stroke, mm	82.0 x 62.0
Equivalent in.	3.23 x 2.44
Displacement, cc/cu in.	3929/240
Compression ratio	10.5:1
Bhp @ rpm, net	325 @ 7500
Equivalent mph	164
Torque @ rpm, lb-ft	260 @ 5500
Equivalent mph	121
Carburetion	six Weber (2V)
Fuel requirement	unleaded, 91-oct

Exhaust-emission control equipment: dual catalytic converters, dual air injection pumps

DRIVETRAIN

Transmission	5-sp manual
Gear ratios: 5th (0.76)	3.11:1
4th (0.99)	4.05:1
3rd (1.31)	5.36:1
2nd (1.77)	7.24:1
1st (2.26)	9.24:1
Final drive ratio	4.09:1

CHASSIS & BODY

Layout	mid engine/rear drive
Body/frame	tubular steel chassis/aluminum panels
Brake system	10.5-in. vented discs front and rear, vacuum assisted
Swept area, sq in.	416
Wheels	Campagnolo cast alloy; 15 x 8½ front, 15 x 12 rear
Tires	Pirelli P7; 205/50VR-15 front, 345/35VR-15 rear
Steering type	rack & pinion
Overall ratio	na
Turns, lock-to-lock	3.0
Turning circle, ft.	38.3

Front suspension: unequal-length A-arms, coil springs, tube shocks, anti-roll bar
Rear suspension: upper lateral links, lower reversed A-arms, upper & lower trailing arms, dual coil springs, dual tube shocks, anti-roll bar

ACCOMMODATION

Seating capacity, persons	2
Seat width, in.	2 x 13.0
Head room	34.0
Seat back adjustment, deg	10

INSTRUMENTATION

Instruments: 320-km/h speedo, 9000-rpm tach, 99,999.9 odo, oil press., oil temp, coolant temp, ammeter, voltmeter, fuel level
Warning lights: brake system, handbrake, alternator, a/c fan, a/c compressor, parking lights, seatbelts, hazard, high beam, directionals

MAINTENANCE

Service intervals, mi:
Oil change	3000
Filter change	3000
Chassis lube	6000
Minor tuneup	6000
Major tuneup	9000
Warranty, mo/mi	none from factory

CALCULATED DATA

Lb/bhp (test weight)	10.0
Mph/1000 rpm (5th gear)	22.5
Engine revs/mi (60 mph)	2670
Piston travel, ft/mi	1085
R&T steering index	1.15
Brake swept area, sq in./ton	256

*Compare the Road & Track profile with the
previous one. Only the space-saver tyre appears
to be missing?*

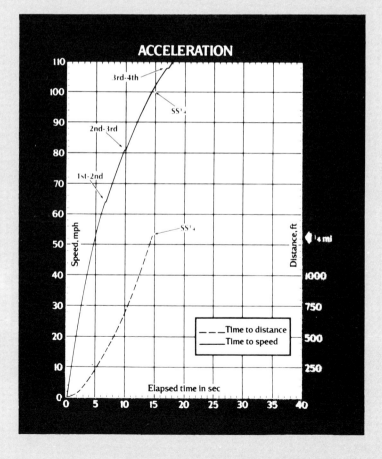

ACCELERATION

Time to distance, sec:

0-100 ft	3.6
0-500 ft	8.7
0-1320 ft (¼ mi)	14.4
Speed at end of ¼ mi, mph	105.5

Time to speed, sec:

0-30 mph	3.7
0-40 mph	4.6
0-50 mph	5.5
0-60 mph	6.8
0-70 mph	8.2
0-80 mph	9.6
0-100 mph	13.3
0-120 mph	18.2

SPEEDS IN GEARS

5th gear (8000 rpm)	192
4th (8000)	155
3rd (8000)	116
2nd (8000)	85
1st (8000)	58

FUEL ECONOMY

Normal driving, mpg	12.0
Cruising range, mi (1-gal. res)	368

HANDLING

Speed on 100-ft radius, mph	35.4
Lateral acceleration, g	0.838
Speed thru 700-ft slalom, mph	60.4

BRAKES

Minimum stopping distance, ft:

From 60 mph	140
From 80 mph	238
Control in panic stop	excellent
Pedal effort for 0.5g stop, lb	18
Fade: percent increase in pedal effort to maintain 0.5g deceleration in 6 stops from 60 mph	nil
Overall brake rating	excellent

INTERIOR NOISE

All noise readings in dBA:

Idle in neutral	73
Maximum, 1st gear	102
Constant 30 mph	77
50 mph	84
70 mph	87
90 mph	91

SPEEDOMETER ERROR

60 km/h (37.3 mph) indicated is actually	38.0
80 km/h (49.7 mph)	50.0
100 km/h (62.1 mph)	62.5
120 km/h (74.6 mph)	75.5
140 km/h (87.0 mph)	89.0

The 5-speed gearbox is a delight for the enthusiast driver—one of the smoothest gated shifters we've ever used, without the notchy feel that marks the operation of the Ferrari 308 GT4 for example. The shift effort is moderately high, as is the clutch pedal pressure. Also the throttle is a bit too stiff, making smooth starts from rest a bit tentative at first.

Entering the Countach is like slipping on a handcrafted, made-to-order Italian shoe—the first time requires thought and planning. First, the highest point on the car is only 42.1 in. above the ground—just about waist high for a 6-footer. Second, the upward pivoting doors reveal an ultra-wide sill that must be negotiated prior to settling into the body-hugging contoured seats. The seats in the S model have provision for back-angle adjustment (about 10 degrees) lacking in earlier models and it's a welcome addition. There isn't an abundance of fore-and-aft adjustment for the driver's seat, but the steering wheel has both tilt and telescopic functions so most every driver will be able to find a comfortable driving position. Anyone more than 6-ft tall, however, will find the car a snug fit, with the only serious problem being lack of head room. Unfortunately the factory installed seatbelts haven't been updated and still get tighter with each movement until they become distinctly uncomfortable.

The interior is handsome and tasteful with leather seats and upholstery, suede trim on the top of the dash and around the windshield and windows, and a headliner of soft, fuzzy white material. It's all appropriately plush as one would expect in a car of this price, and at the same time there is a businesslike aura befitting a superb machine designed for driving near the limits of speed and handling. The instrument panel is reminiscent of an airplane with eight Stewart-Warner gauges and eight warning lights for monitoring the various functions and systems of the car.

There are a few features of the interior arrangement we don't like, such as the glaring flat faces on the gauges, the two (only) center-mounted air conditioning outlets that have limited directional flexibility, and a windshield wiper that interfered with forward vision (especially for the passenger). Rear outward vision, as we noted in our previous road test of the Countach, is severely limited, especially to the quarters, and it takes lots of practice, steely nerves and much care to back up the Lamborghini without a friend outside to assist. Caution is also called for while merging with traffic or changing lanes—and the small rearview mirror along with side windows that only go down some 2 in. don't help.

So, that's the Lamborghini Countach S—still the ultimate exotic car in the world, with styling that makes it one of the most attention-getting cars we've ever driven; performance that, while not as breathtaking as the earlier car, is still sufficient to pump gobs of adrenalin into even the most jaded driver's system; and handling characteristics that nearly defy description. The Countach S is a dream car. Only a handful of very lucky enthusiasts will ever drive one; and even fewer people will ever own one. But that's not the point of the car—it's a monument to automotive design, engineering and enthusiasm . . . a work of art.

Photographic acknowledgements

The vast majority of the photographs used in this book have never been seen before simply because they have been 'saved' until the opportunity of this book presented itself. The late Peter Coltrin and Jean François Marchet have taken years, obviously, to shoot the Countach over the time span of its conception and production. The detail and the outstanding pose of some of the photographs are a lesson to all enthusiasts.

Other photographs were contributed by the various press officers of Automobili Ferruccio Lamborghini SpA, then Nuova Automobili Ferruccio Lamborghini SpA, Fotowall of Bologna, Carrozzeria Bertone SpA, Armin Johl, Jean-Luc Pierre, Patrick Vercher, and Messrs Le Mounier and Charpentier.

Thank you all.

Index

134